Nona Tuscan 29

W9-CPQ-617

HOW TO MAKE SOMETHING
FROM NOTHING

How to Make Something from Nothing

BY

RUTH STEARNS EGGE

COWARD-McCANN, Inc.
NEW YORK

Copyright © 1968 by Ruth Stearns Egge

All rights reserved. This book, or parts thereof, may not be reproduced in any form without permission in writing from the Publisher. Published on the same day in the Dominion of Canada by Longmans Canada Limited, Toronto.

PRINTED IN THE UNITED STATES OF AMERICA

To
FLORENCE K. PALMER
My Friend
of
the Understanding Heart

Acknowledgments

IT IS a pleasure to acknowledge the many friends who have offered their help and have been so gracious as to lend me pieces to photograph.

My wholehearted thanks to Loraine Summers, Ramona Poole, Mrs. R. Simmons, Merle Kirby, Linda Nutter, and Mrs. Larrae Haydon.

The very able photographers who took the pictures for the book—Sherman Washburn, Bill Hupp, Larry Franklin, Ernie Freeman, Josie Barnett, and Jon Egge—deserve particular thanks.

A special acknowledgment to Flo Fields, who conceived the idea of my writing the book and who has given much valuable help and encouragement.

Foreword

THIS book is an offshoot of a hobby that came into being because of a housewifely desire to do something with an attic full of junk—a hobby which has since become an absorbing and profitable craft. In it is a presentation of my knowledge of the subject, learned through experimenting with various methods over a period of years. I hope that you will find as much joy in creation as I have.

Those of you who have a fancy for old things, or love beauty, or just like to work with your hands, will find delight in making something from nothing, and it requires no special talent or expensive tools or anything involving an initial outlay of large sums of money.

This is a hobby that will appeal to anyone interested in distinctive, individual accessories: lamps, candlesticks, wall sconces, and decorator items. There are endless possibilities for making truly beautiful pieces for your home or to give as gifts, from what was previously mere junk.

Contents

Contents

Part III

ON THE PRACTICAL SIDE

Part IV

LET YOURSELF GO

Part I

TREASURE IS WHERE YOU FIND IT

I

Junking...What to Look For

ᴘᴇʀʜᴀᴘs it all began with the first cavewoman who looked at a pile of old bones and hated to throw them away. In my case, however, the pile of bones was an attic full of junk accumulated over the years—a hodgepodge of things that were *too good to throw away.*

At least that's what I told myself—except for moments of doubt experienced each spring and again in the fall, when every glossy page of the home decorator magazines is a challenge to do something about one's own home. *And all those dust catchers in the attic!*

Why not just call the Salvation Army and have them clear out the discards and leftovers of family living? Things that would never be missed—like the old pair of brass andirons, smoke-darkened and green with time; the outdated light fixture, complete with frosted bulbs; and Grandmother's sewing machine; someone said that an old treadle machine makes a good conversation-piece plant stand. There were a couple of bridge lamps, too, the kind popular back in the thirties. And shoved into every corner were tables, chairs, and chests of assorted periods and condition.

What point in saving things you can't use—why take up needed storage space with a lot of junk? But it was "too good to throw away," and I didn't. Then, on a crisp September afternoon, a friend telephoned, suggesting we visit the Home Show, a yearly event in which local merchants and decorators pool their talents to present the latest and loveliest home furnishings. At the Coliseum, the show had been set up in the main arena, with three aisles of model room arrangements. We took our time and studied each exhibit thoroughly but kept wandering back to look at one room in particular— a dining area, styled after an Italian villa (or the way I imagine an Italian villa should look). The colors were lovely; the furniture was carved and beautifully wrought.

The accessories, though, were what caught our attention: softly shaded oversize lamps in a rich, warm brown; an elaborate gold-crested sconce above the marble mantel; vines and gay-colored flowers spilling from a long wooden planter in a casement window. And there on the dining table, arranged for a buffet dinner, stood two magnificent brass candlesticks.

I stared, entranced, yet somewhere in the back of my mind lay the nagging thought that I'd seen them before. Each was massive, more than three feet tall, and consisted of several rounded sections near the base, tapering upward to a gracefully shaped candleholder at the top. Well, one thing was certain, I had never owned anything quite so splendid. I stepped closer to look at the price tag. It almost took my breath away.

Then, as we moved on to another exhibit, it came to me. Those candlesticks—in shape, they reminded me of the brass andirons we'd used in our fireplace for years and recently discarded in favor of new ones. This was the moment when I became a treasure hunter, because I still had those andirons somewhere among the "junk" I should have sent to the Salvation Army—and hadn't.

Of course, their brass finish could be restored with polishing. But could the pair be converted into one tall candlestick? I wondered. As soon as I got home, I brought them down from the attic. Basically, it wasn't such a far-fetched idea, but transforming them into a striking decorator piece was an altogether different matter.

For one thing, the andiron tops were smooth and round, so there was no way of fastening them together. Then, too, instead of an attractive base suitable for a candlestick like the one I'd seen, each had short legs braced by a cast-iron extension. I ransacked the attic for anything that might be usable and found a floor lamp with a few brass sections and a small table lamp with a good brass base.

Having carried these out to the garage, where my husband kept his tools, I studied the andirons again. The first problem was how to get them apart. Eventually, with the aid of two kinds of pliers, I succeeded in loosening a nut at the bottom of one and was surprised to find that it consisted of three separate pieces: the legs; a long center section; and the rounded top. These had given the illusion of being one solid piece before, because a threaded steel rod passed through the hollow center section and into the brass ball on top. This last was screwed onto the rod's end to hold the entire andiron together.

Putting my newfound knowledge to work, I dismantled the second andiron and began on the lamps. Apparently they were made in much the same way, with a rod passing through the center. The only difference in undoing them was that I needed a screwdriver to remove tiny setscrews from the light sockets and wire cutters to snip the wires. When everything was finally apart, and I saw all those lovely brass pieces spread out on the garage floor, it seemed a simple matter to reassemble them in whatever order I chose.

Unfortunately, this was not the case.

To build a candlestick as tall as the one I had in mind, the only rod of the four long enough was the one from the floor lamp—and it was too long by several inches. Besides, it was larger around than the center hole in the andiron parts, although I was able to slip the small-centered pieces onto the more slender table lamp rod. But this wouldn't do either, since the table lamp had been a low one, and its rod was short, the same as the andiron rods. So, there went my plans for a king-size candlestick!

Halfheartedly, I tried two of the andiron middles and a brass part from the floor lamp on the table lamp base. The effect was nice—as far as it went. Taking one of the andiron parts with me for size, I made a fast trip to the nearest hardware store, where an agreeable clerk sold me a rod thirty-six inches long.

Back home once again, I began with the table lamp base, trying the entire assortment of brass pieces, slipping first one, then another over the rod, arranging them this way or that until I had what seemed the right combination. Last of all, a nut went on the top to hold everything in place. But when I showed it to my husband, he shook his head, frowning.

"Crooked—leans to the left," he said and, before I could protest, handed me a pair of pliers. "Here, hold that top nut steady, while I tighten the one at the bottom."

He was right, and my creation was finally done.

That astronomically priced candlestick at the Home Show? Mine was nearly as impressive and had cost exactly $1.09 for the rod, plus a pair of discarded andirons and a couple of useless lamps.

Light-headed with success, I carried it into the house, trying it on the hearth, the coffee table, the window seat in the dining room—my candlestick looked magnificent to me. Anywhere.

From that moment on, I have devoted myself to studying every piece of junk I see with the idea of its potential as building material. Here, as on any treasure hunt, there's always a feeling that just around the corner or in the next shop a fabulous find is waiting.

So, now you are invited to join me in the happy art of *junking,* which, incidentally, isn't in the dictionary. Junking is similar to antique hunting, but it covers a wider range of objects and includes discards to be rejuvenated, as well as the old or rare items. If, in your junking, you happen on to true antiques that can be restored, so much the better. But junk, just the ordinary sort of castoff, is what you'll be looking for and working with most often.

Specifically, you should be on the alert for the following kinds of junk pile treasure:

Old Electrical and Gas Fixtures

There are numerous ways of using bridge lamps, wall fixtures, floor lamps, chandeliers (of almost any period), and all the other endless offshoots of light fixtures. None of these needs to be whole, for it is the parts we are interested in. In time, you'll learn to tell at a glance whether or not there are enough good parts in such a fixture to make it worth your while.

Wood

Nearly everyone is aware that table legs and newel-posts can be made into lovely large candlesticks. But don't overlook other possibilities in wood, such as ornate bits and pieces from antique or near antique furniture; either small or large salad bowls and wooden nut bowls (the better-shaped ones); endpieces from wooden curtain poles; old sewing-machine drawers, and the domed covers from the early machines; interesting flat pieces of wood, perhaps with beveled edges or a bit of carving (sometimes suitable as a background for a sconce); and wooden gingerbread of any kind from old houses.

Wrought and Cast Iron

Be sure to look for ornate or lacy pieces of cast iron, for instance, decorative iron from an old stove (unless there is lettering on it) or any graceful, curved pieces of wrought iron from lighting fixtures, gateposts, and so forth. Avoid wrought iron that has been *welded* together, unless you can use the entire piece as it is, because welding cannot be melted apart with a torch as solder can.

Junk Jewelry

Certain types of jewelry can be used for embellishment or to cover holes. Look for either small or fairly large flat chains; metal (particularly brass) jewelry without stone settings; metal belts, if they have links which can be pried open; bangle jewelry (brass is most desirable, but occasionally other metals or even bangles of colored glass are adaptable).

Glass

There are countless ways of using pretty glass bowls, lamp chimneys, gaslight shades (if you're lucky enough to find any), glass prisms (clear or colored), and railroad lantern chimneys, which come in a lovely blue-green, as well as red.

It might be wise to collect a few glass parts from old lamps in case you decide to build an all-glass candlestick or lamp. Don't overstock on these, however. In regard to candlesticks, the small glass or crystal ones you find in the shops can be greatly enhanced with adapters, a point discussed later on.

Miscellaneous

Look for pans and lids of pleasing shape or size—ones made of fairly lightweight metal so that holes can be drilled in them —also fancy metal curtain and drapery accessories.

This, of course, is not a complete list, and undoubtedly you will uncover other material once your imagination is sparked. For nine years I have built things for gifts at Christmastime, and each new Christmas building spree has yielded some intriguing idea I hadn't considered before.

How to Make Something from Nothing

Prior to starting your search, it might be well to go through this book, chapter by chapter, so you will have a better notion of the kinds of junk to look for.

Also, while you're collecting material, start clipping and saving pictures from magazines and newspapers, of candlesticks, candelabra, wall sconces, compotes, and all types of centerpieces. Pictures do fire the creative instinct. Though you may not wish to copy a particular piece in its entirety, either some portion of it or the way in which it is used may inspire you later on. For instance, the idea of using a floor lamp base as a compote bowl, painting it white and antiquing it in blue, was suggested to me by a color photograph in the food section of a woman's magazine (the centerpiece was featured in a blue and white table setting).

Spend a day, or two or three, at first, junking. This means going from place to place, looking for all sorts of castoffs in your hunt for material. Don't be discouraged if you fail to find anything promising right away. There may be a few dry runs, but soon your eye will become educated to the possibilities latent in all sorts of things.

Usually, it proves more productive and a great deal more fun to take along a friend with a mutual interest in junking. Each of you will see potential in a piece of junk the other has passed by, and one idea may trigger several more. An added bonus will be sharing the excitement over a real find and the hilarity over an occasional dud. There are still a couple of these in my basement which defy all efforts to make them look like anything, but they have provided some good laughs, so they're not a total loss.

Again, don't be surprised if you take home something wildly different from what you had in mind. The best double boiler I ever had, which I still use, came from a secondhand store. So did the mate to one of my antique cups. Don't aim exclusively at finding material for a particular piece. Instead, when you go junking, be flexible, and look around with an open mind to see what is available for transformation.

2

Where to Look

WHY not begin your search in your attic or basement? For instance, tucked away in an attic corner, I found a wedding present lamp with the porcelain smashed beyond repair. Its filigreed metal base later became the foundation for a graceful compote. While rummaging through the family discards, I also uncovered a vintage table. It was bulky and dated but had four exquisitely turned legs, which later made marvelous candlesticks. Explore all your at-home possibilities first. Then, with your senses sharpened, you are ready to tackle the antique, thrift, and secondhand stores.

Often the charitable thrift and salvage shops, such as the ones operated by Goodwill, the Salvation Army, and St. Vincent de Paul are in the same general area, so it is wise to locate addresses in the yellow pages, then to chart your course accordingly. (Large cities have whole sections where the antique, thrift, and secondhand stores are concentrated. For instance, in downtown Seattle, it's in the general area of the Farmers' Market; in New York, Second and Third avenues and Greenwich Village.)

But remember that it's always more fun if you go with someone else. My early junking days were shared with a friend who enjoyed the excitement of exploring junk shops as much as I. We tried always to start early. It's a good idea to arrive as soon after the shops open as possible because dealers make the circuit, too.

Eventually, on these jaunts, we learned to take along a thermos of coffee and some sandwiches. Secondhand stores, unfortunately, are seldom located near a favorite restaurant. Our junking kit also included several pairs of old gloves and a damp washcloth in a plastic bag. (Sooner or later, as we became more and more absorbed in our treasure hunt, we invariably forgot to put on the gloves.)

Usually, among our first stops were the "as is" departments of local thrift shops. Turnover is rapid here, and almost anything may be uncovered on the heaped tables—lamps, dishes, picture frames, automotive parts, clocks, small electrical appliances, pots and pans, vintage light fixtures, or what have you. Admittedly, much of the junk appears worthless—at least for your purpose—and there will be times when you'll swear they ought to send it all straight to the dump. But we have found it pays to be persistent. There always comes a day when you *do* find something good.

On such a day, our haul might include several table lamps with good bases, perhaps some parts from a discarded wall or overhead light fixture, a table leg, and a drawer from an old sewing machine, or a handful of putting-together material, such as metal washers, nuts, and threaded lamp rods.

If we were lucky, we might even find a complete light fixture or a usable floor lamp with a not-too-large base. On our first trips, everything was carefully scrutinized as prospective material, but after we'd acquired a little more experience, we were able to scan the merchandise quickly and judge what was practical. In this way we covered a lot of places. Whatever each store had to offer was soon stowed away in the back of the car, and off we'd go again, completely caught up in our search—so excited, in fact, that we could scarcely wait to see what might be waiting for us at the next stop.

You'll undoubtedly discover that certain shops will become your favorites. For example, even those operated by Goodwill or St. Vincent de Paul vary in different parts of the country. Some sell their scrap metal (including light fixtures) directly to a junkyard dealer and, therefore, will have little to offer. Others will be abundant sources of the articles you are looking for.

Taken as a whole, however, the shops you'll want to visit most often are ones that cater to the do-it-yourself trade or ones where the stock is constantly changing.

In the summertime, an antique shop or perhaps several of them together may hold a stock-thinning sale, sometimes referred to as an outdoor sale. Near antiques, damaged pieces, and all sorts of interesting odds and ends are offered at reasonable prices. Such sales are great fun and offer exactly the kind of merchandise you're looking for.

And don't overlook the various kinds of auctions as an excellent source of supply. These are advertised in the classified section of your newspaper and by display ads in the main news pages. Storage companies often hold warehouse sales to clear out abandoned goods or freight with unpaid charges against it. Some companies, too, sell secondhand household goods, screening out antiques for special auction. And when handsome old buildings or hotels are to be torn down, their contents and furnishings are sometimes sold at auction as well.

Colleges, libraries, and historical societies occasionally sponsor auctions when the contents of estates (or the proceeds therefrom) are willed to them. So do art galleries. And like homemakers, they clean house, sorting out things that aren't of gallery quality to dispose of at auction. There are also auction houses which do nothing but accept odd lots from private parties or estates to auction off. One such sale may include furnishings from several small estates or just one or two collections from a very large one. These houses also handle imported goods that are shipped into the country specifically to be auctioned.

People have long been fascinated by country auctions where farms or old family homes and their furnishings are sold. There is a special atmosphere about this sort of sale, particularly when the weather is nice. Besides, country auctions are noted for turning up rare bargains, doubtless accounting for their popularity. Watch for announcements of country auctions in suburban or small-town newspapers. Often larger auctions are advertised in the city papers.

Equally popular, however, are the suburban garage sales, now a part of the American scene, in which one person or a group of friends will assemble a conglomeration of items and run an ad in the local newspaper under "Miscellaneous." Based on the idea that everyone loves to go through someone else's junk, the garage sale gives every promise of being with us for a long, long time. It offers all the value of a bargain basement, only with a bit more class and a lot more fun. Nor are these sales confined to a particular income group. On any weekend—from Thursday on—homemade signs proclaiming GARAGE SALE can be seen sprouting from lawns of homes in modest developments or elegant old residential neighborhoods. Often there may be several sales in one block.

Most of the people who hold garage sales also love to attend them, and this makes for a lively exchange, the bait, of course, being bargains in antiques—which, indeed, are the focal part of the picture. But a sale may include a great variety of inexpensive objects, anything from a ten-cent coaster set or fifteen-cent mixing bowl to a one-dollar frame or two-dollar table.

Men also turn up at garage sales, displaying particular interest in sports equipment, guns, and antiques. All sale items are marked, and prices are reasonable. Very little bargaining is done, and customers who decide to think it over and come back later are almost certain to find the article gone.

In many cities, there are now specialty shops that deal only in secondhand material from wrecked buildings. You may have to turn detective to find these, but it's worth it. Dealers who sell this kind of salvage may be listed in the yellow pages under "Antiques," "Salvage," or "Used Building Material." Their stock may include anything from an ancient tub to pieces of handsomely carved wood. The wreckers will not always deal with small-scale buyers. Occasionally, however, you may find one who will let you go through the old house he is demolishing and buy what you want for a small price. In one of these houses I found a carved massive newel-post encrusted with the natural grime of fifty years. It eventually became a tall candlestick for my Christmas hearth. Check your newspaper under "Miscellaneous for Sale." Some wreckers advertise salvage material when they start to tear down an old house.

The easiest way to clean up such wood or metal is to have it stripped professionally by steam. In areas where this service is available, it will be listed in the yellow pages under "Steam Cleaning (Industrial and Commercial)." Removing paint and varnish is their specialty, but these firms often have bits of interesting old wood and metal for sale, as well as furniture already cleaned of varnish or paint. In addition to the steam strippers, there are, in some cities, small shops that specialize in stripping by other means—similar to the methods suggested in Chapter 10.

A trip to a lamp shop will really inspire you and can provide a marvelous source of supplementary material—lamp parts, prisms, bobeches, chimneys, to mention only a few. This kind of shop may be listed under "Lampshades and Lamps (Custom Made)." It makes lamps to order but will also sell you the parts that enable you to make your own.

Any hardware store can supply two important items on your putting-together list, unless there is already a good supply of them among your junk:

(1) Lamp rods, 3/8 inch. They come in short pieces (2 or 3 inches), as well as in 3-foot lengths. (2) Steel nuts. (Brass ones are fine, too, but more expensive.) The trade terms used to designate size are confusing, so just ask the clerk for steel nuts that will fit on a 3/8-inch lamp rod.

It will add spice to your junking trip if you investigate an antique shop or two along the way. They may have prisms, bowls, glass candlesticks, or shades, any one of which could prove to be the very thing you need to enhance a particular creation. You might even want to buy an attractive bowl, then build a base to set it in. (Plate 1.)

PLATE 1. Brass base by the author (*left*). Made up of six separate parts, the base is polished brass. It complements a cut-glass bowl. The small pair of candlesticks (*right*) was made by the author for Merle Kirby of Milwaukie, Oregon. These, too, are composed of several small brass pieces, all of which were buffed and polished before being assembled.

Or on—as shown in Plate 2—as an extra precaution, florist's clay has been placed around the top rim of the base—at the point of contact with the bowl's convex glass bottom. (Roll the clay first between your palms till it forms a slender ropelike piece. Then circle it atop the rim, and set the bowl down on it.)

By the way, when buying florist's clay, choose the kind sold in florist's shops. You can get the same type at other stores, too, but check for quality before you overstock, since some clay is aggravatingly sticky and difficult to handle.

But to get back to our search for material—once in a while you may hit the jackpot and discover a real bargain at a church or school rummage sale. Watch your newspaper for rummage sale notices (under "Miscellaneous"). You are also apt to find, under this heading, ads for damaged and unclaimed freight. Occasionally, the freight company will have a few lamps or parts of lamps for sale.

After several years of scouting our local thrift shops, my friend and I decided to try our luck farther afield. So we chose a large city about 200 miles away, planning on four days, a full day for the trip, two days to do the stores, and a day to drive back.

It isn't so much *where* you go that makes extended junking safaris exciting adventure. A good share of it is anticipation—that, and the fun of discovering new shops, especially along the way. For this reason, you'll want to allow ample traveling time, in order to leave the highway at various places and drive through each town of any size. (By asking at service stations for locations of Salvation Army or Goodwill stores, you can pinpoint general areas of interest.)

On a long trip it's a good idea to take apart some of your

PLATE 2. White centerpiece built by the author for Loraine Summers of Milwaukie, Oregon, is set off by yellow candles in pale-green vigil cups, and a sunny Vaseline-glass bowl. The wrought iron was put together by hand, using tiny bolts and epoxy.

bulkier finds—tables, sewing machines, floor lamps, and the like—in order to make more room.

The first time, of course, we went unprepared, so when the junk we'd collected (floor lamps, assorted electrical fixtures, the top of an old parlor organ, part of an oak dresser, and an antique chair), threatened to crowd us out of the car, we borrowed some tools from our motel proprietor and dismantled what we could on the spot.

Nowadays on out-of-town trips I always carry a screwdriver, pliers, and wire cutters in my purse. A word of caution, however—if you dismantle anything en route, be sure to save all the nuts and bolts removed. They may be worth the weight of a bulging purse when it comes to creating a treasure from the junk you collect.

Remember, though, just because it's fun to explore new shops doesn't mean that the junking is bound to be better far from home. You'll find most of the places mentioned in this chapter right in your own community. Each is a reliable source of material, and you can go back regularly, as the stock changes or your ideas expand.

3
Junk into Building Material

Y̲OU'VE been junking. You have your own junk pile. So what do you do with it?

Working Space

First, of course, you find a corner and a stout table where you can work. The table should provide enough room to enable you to lay out the various pieces, so that you can ponder and take your time in designing. If possible, reserve this spot for your craft and use the space under the table for storage. In a garage or basement, much of your material can be hung overhead or on the wall, where it can be seen and is readily accessible.

An apartment-dwelling friend of mine has arrived at a

rather neat solution to her junk-storage problem. After comb-
ing the Goodwill and secondhand stores, she found an old
five-drawer highboy chest—one that was sturdily built and had
smooth-sliding drawers. She painted it, then installed it in a
corner of the eating area adjacent to her kitchenette. In a
nearby closet she keeps a folding card table and a small
plastic drop cloth. Her junk is dismantled as soon as she
brings it into the apartment and is then stored compactly in
the chest of drawers, along with her pliers and other tools.

She can whisk out the drop cloth, set up the card table, and
all her equipment is right there, ready to go. Naturally, she
scales building, as well as buying, to the space in which she
must work. In a later chapter I'll tell you about one of her
most fascinating card table construction projects. It's one I
think you may want to try—a colored glass window that is
simply beautiful.

But for now let's consider your own stockpile of potential
building material.

Equipment

Gather the tools and supplies that you need to begin:
Cotton gloves (I buy old cotton ladies' gloves at the salvage
store. These can be thrown in the washer. Gardening gloves
are too bulky.)
Hammer
Pliers (two pairs)
Wire cutters, old shears, or tin snips
Screwdrivers (two—one large and one small)
Penetrating oil
Paint thinner and remover
Scouring pads

Small magnet—for testing metals
Epoxy glue
Good all-purpose glue
Medium-size vise

Method

Put on the pair of old gloves, and begin taking your junk apart. As you do so, notice the way the lamps or lighting fixtures are fastened together and how the different parts are built up to form the complete fixture. By doing this, you'll gain some tips on construction that will serve you well when it comes to creating your own designs.

In dismantling, use wire cutters or shears to snip all electric wires. Next, with a pair of pliers in each hand, one to grip or hold and the other to work with, unscrew each nut and anything else that will come apart. Wherever nuts, bolts, or screws are badly rusted and almost impossible to loosen, apply a little penetrating oil, and allow some time for it to do its work before trying again with pliers and screwdriver. (More than one application may be needed; be sure to clean off all traces of oil afterward with paint thinner.)

Should you happen on to a few pieces that have been soldered, lay them aside (unless usable as they are) until you can get someone to melt the solder for you. After operating in this fashion for a couple of years, I bought an inexpensive small propane torch for this purpose.

For myself, as well as my hobby-conscious friends, it has always been a thrill to see how much useful building material can be salvaged from a few castoffs.

Every ring and nut should be stockpiled. And when taking a lamp apart, don't throw away the light sockets. In addition to their normal function, they have many other uses. For instance, the lower portion of a socket—or cap—which is threaded, can take the place of a nut on the bottom end of your lamp rod (inside the base) to hold your creation together.

If necessary, you can also compress these caps in order to make them more compact. Place the cap on your workbench; then hit the threaded end with a hammer, forcing it downward and into the cap itself. I've even used light socket caps for small candleholders, by adding a ring or washer underneath and a small decorative chain (from a bracelet or necklace) around their rims.

As a rule, I discard the china or pottery parts of a lamp, although occasionally there'll be one I want to save. For example, I once bought a lamp strictly for its base, but it had very attractive lines and was quite large. For a long time it languished undismantled in a corner of my basement. Then one day I desperately needed a lamp to replace one that had been broken. Bringing it upstairs, I painted and antiqued the shabby old relic and contrived a shade. To this day, it's among my favorite lamps.

Now, about the varying sizes of rods you will find in your junk and how to adapt them to your projects. You may have noticed while dismantling lamps and light fixtures that sometimes two pieces of rod may be joined by a short coupling (Figure 1c), often made of brass and threaded inside.

Or possibly you will find a coupling used in combination with a reducing bushing. These bushings come in various sizes and are threaded *inside and out,* enabling you to join two different-sized rods or to fit the small threaded stem of a candleholder neatly into a larger hole. (Figure 2b.)

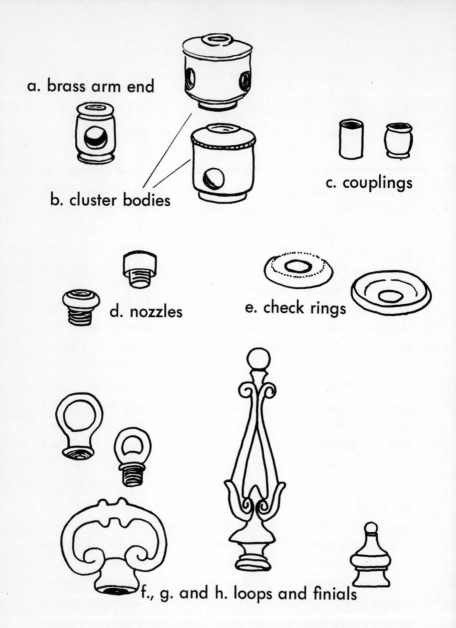

a. brass arm end

b. cluster bodies

c. couplings

d. nozzles

e. check rings

f., g. and h. loops and finials

FIGURE 1. Small, useful building parts found on secondhand lighting fixtures, table lamps, floor lamps, and wall and ceiling fixtures.

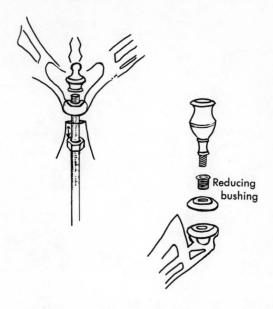

Reducing
bushing

FIGURE 2. a. Shows construction of contemporary candelabra (Plate 7). b. Detail of candle cups on same candelabra illustrates use of reducing bushing in fitting a small rod into a larger hole.

Other versatile building aids that are likely to be found in your raw material are shown in Figure 1. Some of the ways in which they can implement your decorative designs will be brought out in later chapters.

But right now, let's look at two of the "before" items pictured in Plate 3 to see what building parts they contain and how these might be used. For instance, look at Number 4. This particular piece, in addition to the usual putting-to-gether material, such as a rod, screws, nuts, and light sockets, yields the following treasure: three curved pieces of wrought iron, similar in shape to pieces used for the candelabrum in

PLATE 3. Raw material for construction: Numbers 1, 6, 11, and 17 are old electrical wall brackets; Numbers 2, 3, 4, 5, and 10 are ceiling fixtures or parts from them; Numbers 7 and 14 are table legs; Number 12 is the cast-iron top from a parlor heating stove; Number 13 is a wrought-iron curlicue; Numbers 15 and 19 are the top and bottom of an aluminum silex coffeepot; Number 16 is a pottery lamp; Number 18 is the carved front of a cuckoo clock; Number 20 is a piece of cast iron, with the top of the design broken off; and Number 21 is a metal ornament for the top of a heating stove (removed from Number 12).

Plate 24, and three fancy loops much like those on the wall sconce in Plate 4.

The round central portion of the fixture with its attractive ropelike edging could be turned upside down to make an interesting bowl for a centerpiece.

Our second castoff is Number 3 in the photograph. Disassembled, it produces a twelve-inch threaded rod, assorted nuts and building rings, a coupling, and six brass loops that are usable in a variety of ways as trim or for hangers. The large star-shaped portion of the fixture, which is pot metal, could make an attractive wall sconce—perhaps by adding an arm to each of the three lower points in the design and hanging the finished sconce from the fourth and topmost point. The gracefully curving, stem-like extension on top of the fixture originally served to suspend it from the ceiling, in place of a chain. Only partially visible in the photograph, this extension consists of three separate brass parts. Two of these, a bell-shaped part and a small middle part, are like those used for a base and middle on the candelabra in Plates 5 and 6. The third is similar to the pyramidlike pieces of brass built into the contemporary candelabrum and candleholder with hurricane shade in Plate 7.

The handsome finial might be used to create a potpourri jar lid, such as the ones in Plate 19, while the four ornamental flanges (framing the light sockets) would serve as charming candleholders on almost any sizable candlestick or candelabrum. (A metal ring or washer is used to reduce the large opening in the center.)

As for candleholders, I'm partial to metal flowers. These can be bought new at some lamp stores where they make lamps to order, and occasionally an antique or secondhand store will have them, particularly those do-it-yourself shops

PLATE 4. Wall sconce by the author. Although the back of this sconce appears to be carved wood, it is actually cast iron from an old cookstove, combined with a curved piece of beveled wood found in a junkyard.

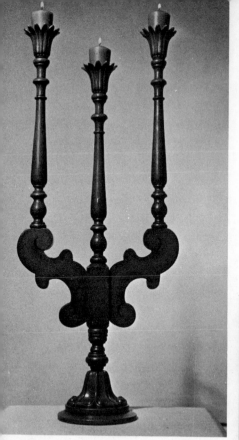

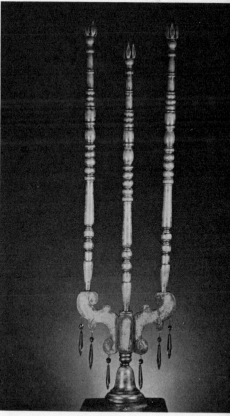

PLATE 5. Wooden candelabrum by the author utilizes slender balustrade posts, part of an old table, and metal parts from a secondhand store light fixture.

PLATE 6. Contemporary wooden candelabrum by Margaret Haydon of Milwaukie, Oregon, has base and candle cups of metal. Its center section is carpenter-cut antique table legs, and the entire piece is finished in white and gold, set off by crystal prisms.

PLATE 7. Contemporary pieces made by the author. The one on the left combines brass and painted surfaces. The piece on the right is polished brass with an amber glass chimney.

which deal in secondhand material for handicraft projects—
old wood, parts of furniture, metal pieces, and so on.

While metal flowers are very pretty, however, they aren't
necessarily the only or the best choice for everything you
build. As an example, in Plate 45, the candelabrum on the
left would, I think, be improved so far as design is concerned
by substituting a different type of candleholder—something a
bit flatter and less ornate.

Incidentally, if your metal flowers are not constructed of
too heay a metal, it is possible to reshape them. (Figure 3.)
The ones I'm referring to are those that are fairly good-sized

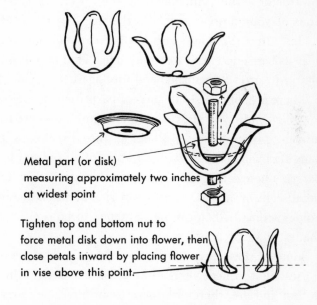

Metal part (or disk)
measuring approximately two inches
at widest point

Tighten top and bottom nut to
force metal disk down into flower, then
close petals inward by placing flower
in vise above this point.

FIGURE 3. Reshaping metal flowers.

but not adequately shaped to hold a vigil cup. To correct this fault, open them out as flat as possible with your hands (or turn them upside down and use a hammer). Now search through your supply of metal pieces for a circular part or ring the same size as the *bottom of a vigil cup*. Naturally, it must be one with a center hole and made of fairly stout metal. Place it inside the flower, and insert a short length of lamp rod (two or three inches), extending the rod through the flower's center as well. Add a nut at each end of the rod, and tighten both with pliers till your circle of metal is forced down inside the flower as far as it will go without tilting to one side.

The reshaping is done last—by squeezing tops of petals on opposing sides together (preferably in a vise) and inward toward the center, thus bending the lower, less flexible portions of your flower's petals to the shape of the inner metal circlet. Once the flower cup has been rebent and broadened near its base enough to accommodate a vigil cup, it is a simple matter to spread open the petal tops again.

There are, of course, all sorts of parts that can be converted to hold candles or glass containers, and while we're on the subject, notice (also in Plate 3) the three cups that are hanging from chains attached to part of an old fixture (Number 5). These can be transformed into versatile candleholders, because built in along their top rim at intervals are shade holder screws, which can be tightened to hold either gaslight shades or small bowls.

Some of these cups have a large hole in one side to allow for the light socket switch. Others, like the ones in the picture, do not and are, therefore, more desirable. They may also be adapted as middles in candlesticks or decorator pieces by the

PLATE 8. The secondhand and thrift shops are a junker's paradise: Number 1 is a brass ceiling fixture (painted over); Number 2 is a silvered brass chandelier; Number 3 is a ceiling canopy (covers wiring and ceiling hanger); Numbers 5 and 8 are brass floor lamp arms; Number 6 is a central cluster body with brass arms; Number 7 is a light fixture part; Number 9 is a Syrocowood ashtray; Number 10 is a lamp with cast-iron base; Number 11 is a metal pinup light; Number 12 is a wooden ornament from an old building; and Number 13 is a pottery lamp.

addition of a succeeding part large enough to cover the top opening.

Remember, these are only suggestions, and—I can't stress this enough—there is always more than one way to use practically anything that is usable at all. Just for fun, sometime, ask three of your friends how each would utilize a particular castoff or part, and you're likely to get three widely dissimilar but equally usable answers.

But again, how you decide to use any specific part will be dictated by your individual taste. For example, first take a look at the "before" picture of a floor lamp top (Plate 8, Number 4). I happened on to an identical pair of these in a secondhand store, and since I'm not partial to pairs of anything, they presented an interesting challenge in working out separate designs for each. (Plates 45 and 7.) Both pieces are detailed in Chapter 9.

Now, before you start your project, determine whether or not your building material requires further preparation.

Cleaning

A good many of these old things need only scrubbing and cleaning to put them in shape. Some call for scouring pads and paint remover (see Chapter 10).

Wooden or metal pieces that have heavy varnish or chipped paint should be sanded or stripped. Remember, in this connection, the steam cleaning establishments. As a rule they charge according to the size of the object. (I had several coats of paint and varnish removed from Grandmother's old rocker for approximately two dollars.)

If you're working with brass, you may eventually want to have these parts commercially buffed and polished, but it is best to wait and see if they are to be part of your final design.

Brass pieces are sometimes hard to recognize if they have been painted over or plated with silver. Keep a small magnet on your workbench for testing metals. (I take one along when I go junking, too.) Brass and copper do not magnetize, whereas cast iron does. Pot metal will not magnetize either, but it is much lighter weight and has an entirely different feel to it from cast brass.

Occasionally, brass plating, over iron or pot metal, may look like solid brass. If in doubt, take a knife or some sharp object, and make a few scratches in the metal to see if it is the same color (brass) underneath.

All this is not nearly as complicated as it sounds, nor will it make any difference what kind of metal it is, unless you're especially interested in brass and copper. I concentrated exclusively on brass at first and was perpetually on the lookout for it, but now I prefer painting and antiquing as a finish for most of my things.

Additional equipment (as needed):*

Metal file
Hacksaw

If your junk contains a number of wooden pieces, you may need:

Drill
Saw
Assortment of wood screws
Wood rasp

In the beginning, ordinary household tools will do. For the first year and a half, my own handicraft kit consisted of

---

* Don't rush out to buy every item on the list. You can acquire them as you work.

three pairs of pliers, two screwdrivers, a pair of tin snips, and some wire cutters. That's why I emphasize the fact that this craft is very adaptable. It can be gratifyingly simple or can expand to become as creatively complex as you wish to make it.

Each new piece you build is likely to be different from the one before, yet there is a basic principle of construction that will be described in the ensuing chapters and can be followed step by step.

Part II
ACCENT ON CANDLELIGHT

4

Let's Build a Candlestick

Now we come to the fun of building. No matter how lavish the design, the method is the same. It is remarkably simple, too. Do you remember, in Chapter 1, how the andiron candlestick was put together? Its construction is typical. *Nearly everything you build will have a lamp rod as a backbone.*

Again, let's take a candlestick as a graphic example and do a more detailed run-through of the basic principle. For a candlestick, say 15 inches tall, your first requirement will be a lamp rod approximately that long. (This does not hold true for a table leg candlestick, where a slightly different method is used.)

When you are beginning, it is easier to use a standard lamp rod, 3/8 inch (outside diameter)—one that is threaded along its entire length. Don't throw away the odd-sized, partially threaded rods from your junk, however; you can use them later. You will also need two steel or brass nuts to fit on your 3/8-inch lamp rod.

To go back to the basic principle, it is similar to threading beads on a knotted string. Think of the lamp rod as the string, the separate parts of your candlestick as beads, and the nuts (one for each end of the rod) as the knotted ends.

First, screw one of the nuts onto the lamp rod. Add the base of your choice, then the center portion, and finally, the crown. If the assemblage meets with your approval, add the second nut at the top, and tighten both ends with the pliers. It's as easy as that.

You may want to build a massive candlestick or a short, fat one, but whatever the size, it is assembled in exactly the same way. This principle will be applied to more elaborate creations later on, so it should be kept in the back of your mind both when you select your junk and when you design.

As far as designing goes, there is no limit to what you can do. Try various bases, tops, and middles. Slip each piece onto the rod; then choose the ones that go together well and are pleasing to the eye. Should you happen to have several parts that are duplicates, try inserting them at various points in your candlestick. The repetition of a single motif can do wonders to unify your design. (Plate 9.)

The more ways in which a candlestick—or anything else you build—can be used, the greater will be your enjoyment of it. For instance, the fat little candlestick in Plate 10 can double as a base for a shade or a bowl, as shown in Plate 11. And in order to bring about still another change, prisms can be suspended from holes in the rim of the top.

Where actual construction is concerned, a common fault

PLATE 9. Table leg candlestick with oval cast-iron base by Carol Simmons. With the exception of its metal base and three scalloped metal flanges, this piece was made entirely of wood, including its salad bowl top.

PLATE 10. This small, stocky candlestick by the author can double as the base for a gaslight shade or bowl (see Plate 11, left side).

PLATE 11. Candlestick by the author (*left*). The addition of a fluted gaslight shade to the smaller candlestick and an amber glass chimney to the one on the right lends a touch of glamor.

lies in using an overlarge base, such as one from an old *wooden* floor lamp. These are usually too flat as well, so that no matter how attractively the finished piece is painted, it's apt to wind up looking like a sawed-off floor lamp. The size of your base will dictate the height of your candlestick. You'll get better at judging scale as you go along. (Some of my earlier creations looked sadly out of proportion to me later on.)

And how do you decide what to use for bases, center sections, and tops? Let us consider these in relation to our candlestick:

Base

The bottom of the candlestick may be wood or metal or both. It can be a single part (such as an old lamp base), or it can be made up of pieces put together to form a composite—as in Figure 4.

Middle Portion

You will seldom find a single piece which is long enough or exactly the right shape to use by itself. Rather, you will combine a number of parts to make up the center portion. Such parts, depending on their size and shape, are correctly termed columns, necks, founts, breaks, or spindles. But for simplicity's sake we will classify them all as middles.

It is possible to copy the general shape or contour of one particular building part even though you haven't a single piece like it in your collection. Here too, the composite approach is used. For example, let's take a chunky middle part like the one built into the short candlestick in Plate 10. Alternate ways of ultimately achieving the same result are

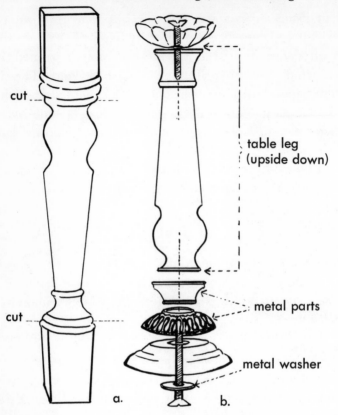

cut

table leg
(upside down)

cut

metal parts

metal washer

a.   b.

FIGURE 4. How to construct a composite base for a table leg candlestick. This one is composed of both wood and metal parts.

illustrated in Figure 5. (Just keep the overall outline in
mind, and try different parts in combination until they add
up to approximately the shape of the piece you want.)

Top

Again, the top, or crown, may be only one part, or it may
be several, piled one on top of another. In fact, I like to

FIGURE 5. How composite middle parts are built up to achieve any desired shape.

finish off a candlestick with a series of pieces, perhaps a cup with one or two rather flat platelike parts in graduated sizes, underneath.

If you should choose as a top for your candlestick a decorative metal flange (one that has a large center hole), you'll need to cover this opening with a metal check or seating ring (see Figure 1e). These have a half-turned-under rolled edge. It is sometimes advisable to depress the center of such a ring so that when a nut is added it will remain level with the top in the event you want to set a vigil cup on it. To depress: Lay the ring on your workbench, inside down, and give a few sharp raps in the center with a hammer.

A part can often be used in a variety of ways. Try it first as a top, then as a middle. Try it right side up and upside down. (I guess this is what my husband was referring to when he said, "Your craft is hardly an exact science.") You needn't be quite this flexible, but don't be afraid to experiment. Be daring. It will surprise you to discover how spectacular your creations can be.

Each candlestick of the small pair that was made to match the jewel box in Plate 12 consists of just three main pieces (plus the usual building rings and so on). The two bases I found on a pair of flimsy-looking lamps about a foot tall that were made up of semiflat glass pieces with metal rings between—the kind of fixture that used to be called a boudoir lamp. There is a small wooden middle in each candlestick (also from such a lamp), and the pot metal flower tops came from an old wall bracket.

In building a tall candlestick, try to break up long sections of the center column by inserting flat or slightly cupped pieces at intervals. The large black candlestick and the two gilt ones in Plate 13 may sere as catalysts here. And if your junk contains only a few such parts, you can almost always find something of similar shape—for instance, small lids with holes drilled in them (perhaps ornamented with metal chain), wooden disks, or individual Jell-o molds.

Building Aids

Right here is a good place to mention that extra something you can do to your candlestick to give it a sturdy, well-put-together look. Remember all those metal rings and washers you found when taking apart your junk?

As you will recall, they were originally used *between* the larger pieces to make them fit snugly, one against the other.

PLATE 12. Jewel box mended and restored by the author. The candle-sticks, constructed from secondhand material, were refinished, as was the jewel box, in white and gold. The box is lined with turquoise silk, and candles of the same color are used in the candleholders.

PLATE 13. Floor candlesticks by the author. The one on the left has, superimposed on its base, a lightweight piece of scrolled metal (probably from some sort of Mexican artware). All three candlesticks were constructed according to the basic method from numerous small parts.

They are also invaluable rebuilding aids. (You can buy new rings and washers in assorted sizes, but look for them in secondhand hardware sections as well.)

Finishing Steps

Your candlestick is now almost complete except for a bit of finishing, and most of this is optional, depending on how much of it you care to do. Some pieces require no more than a quick coat of spray paint or a light brushing with gilt. Others, you may want to paint and antique (see Chapter 10). It will improve the appearance of your project if you cover any noticeable screw holes or joinings. This is where the little ornamental touches described in Chapter 11 are added.

If you decide to paint your candlestick, you may wish to do so before or after you add the ornaments. This depends on whether you want them to stand out as contrast or to blend into the background.

Your creation looks fine, but how does it feel? If it lacks sufficient weight for balance, add some plaster of paris or tile-setting compound in the inside hollow of the base and allow it to dry.

The final step involves scratchproofing the base. There is, on the market, a felt-textured paper with adhesive backing which is the ultimate in convenience. You may, however, want to cushion the base of your candlestick by making use of ladies' felt hats bought at salvage stores. They can be found in every imaginable color (to match any paint job), and each hat will yield more than enough material for one article. Cover the entire bottom of the base, or just glue a rim of felt around the edge—whichever way you prefer. But first take the hat's brim and crown apart. Then, if you intend covering the base completely, cut out a circle of felt. Never mind if the center is cupped; it will flatten out as soon as the felt is glued to the plaster of paris, wood, or whatever.

When it's dry, put your candlestick on the mantel and admire it. Now aren't you glad you didn't throw that junk away?

5
Utilizing Wood

E VEN after being painted and antiqued, wood—more than
most materials—tends to retain the handcrafted look.
Better yet, wood is extremely adaptable. One reason for this
is the ease with which holes can be drilled, enabling one to
attach wrought iron or other metals in order to create unusual designs. See Plates 25 and 26. We will explore this
sort of construction later.

But first let's see what can be done with a few of the common everyday pieces that you are likely to encounter.

Table Legs

No doubt you've seen candlesticks made from table legs
or perhaps balustrade posts in Christmas displays and garden

shows, so you may already have a fairly good idea of how they are put together. But for those who are not chronic pokers and priers into the secrets of such lovely changelings, here is the key to creating equally dramatic candlesticks or candelabra from junk.

Let's assume that the table leg you want to use has been removed from its top, and you are now ready to begin building. It may give your candlestick a more interesting line if you turn the leg upside down, but whichever end is used, a hole must be drilled in the bottom. The base, if not too heavy, can then be attached with a long flatheaded screw—one slightly longer than the depth of the hole and a bit larger in diameter so that it will hold well in the wood. Or for a base that is heavy, drill a larger hole in the table leg, and instead of the screw, glue in a length of lamp rod (as in the wooden candelabrum, Chapter 6).

A nicely proportioned table leg may need only a base to become a true decorator piece. Simple table leg creations such as this can be most impressive with a large candle and perhaps a spray of holly or other greenery for accent.

If you prefer a more finished candleholder, however, it might improve your design to saw off the squared portions of one, or both, ends of the table leg before you begin to build. But that's up to your own creative imagination and part of what makes each new project an exciting game. And should you decide this particular candlestick needs a top, it can be fastened to the leg as illustrated in Figure 4.

When choosing a base, be selective. Those from old floor lamps are often too heavy for this sort of construction, and you'll probably find that a smaller base is better-looking, as well as more practical. It isn't always easy to find one exactly the right size, though, so here is what you can do. Suppose

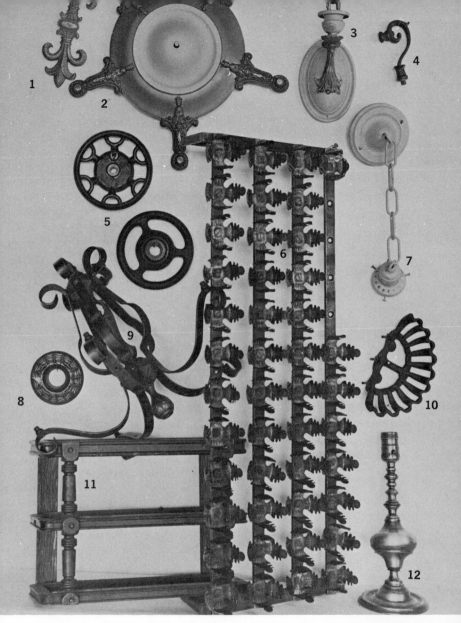

PLATE 14. Treasure ready for conversion: Number 1 is a metal curtain tieback; Number 2 is part of a brass light fixture; Number 3 is a brass wall light; Number 4 is the cast-iron arm from a wall fixture; Number 5, wheels from sewing-machine heads; Number 6, metal flowers screwed onto a steel frame; Number 7 is a shade holder encircling a light socket (attached to a chain and ceiling canopy); Number 8 is an ornamental light socket flange; Number 9 is a wrought-iron chandelier; Number 10 is a cast-iron part from an old-fashioned clothes rack; Number 11 is the framework for sewing-machine drawers; and Number 12 is a small metal table lamp.

you unearth an ornate metal flange in that pile of junk, resembling the one in Plate 14, Number 8. By itself, the flange is not large enough to serve as a base for anything very tall. Yet if it is superimposed over a plain and otherwise uninteresting wood or metal base (see Figure 14), the small part gains both size and importance and, once painted, will appear to be a single piece. This same procedure can be used on any lamp base that is off scale for your purpose.

In regard to table legs, here is a thought you may find useful. A cabinetmaker who has helped me with many a project evolved his own method for putting a hole through table legs and posts, making them much more usable for lamps and such. Since it is by no means easy to drill a straight hole through a lengthy hardwood table leg, he saws the leg completely in half (the long way) with an electric saw, then routs out a rounded groove down the center of each half leg, and glues the two halves together. Presto! A table leg with a perfectly straight hole through the middle.

For me, the neatly cut halves he turned out sparked another idea, that of using the half table legs as backs for sconces. (Plate 15.) With wrought-iron arms and candleholders added, these make unusual and elegant wall pieces. (See Chapter 15.)

Simplicity of construction appeals to most women, whereas a man with his added know-how and extra knowledge of skill tools can build more complex pieces—and with greater ease.

As for myself, I am likely to get ideas that exceed my capabilities. Fortunately, there are always carpenters and cabinetmakers available who can in a pinch do miraculous things to a piece of wood.

At this point I suggest that if you plan on working with wood to any extent, you scout around for a drill, (preferably

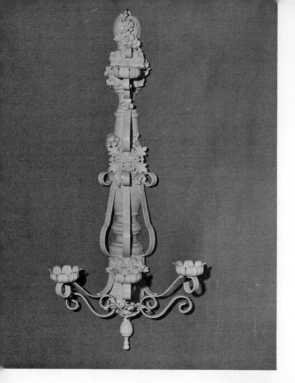

PLATE 15. Wooden table leg sconce by the author. The sconce has wrought-iron arms and flower candleholders that were found on an old chandelier. Tiny metal flowers and ornaments have been added for interest, as well as to camouflage construction details. This sconce is shown decorated for Christmas in Plate 63.

PLATE 16. Victorian wall piece by the author. Made from the remains of an old parlor organ. Missing wooden knobs and finials have been replaced with metal ones, and the whole piece is sprayed stark white.

an electric one) and some bits in various sizes, from 1/8 up
to and including 7/16, which is the right size to accommodate
a lamp rod. Otherwise, perhaps you can recruit someone to
drill the necessary holes. At any rate, never try to fasten a
screw into wood without first drilling a hole—you may split
the wood. (Before drilling any hole in wood or metal, always
make a slight indentation with a nail and hammer so the drill
will be sure to stay on target.) I have a friend who tactfully
persuades her husband to do the manual labor while she does
the designing. The arrangement works well, too. Between
them, they've completed so many decorative items that they
have now begun to sell them.

Parts and Pieces of Old Furniture

The Victorian wall piece shown in Plate 16 was built
from the ornate top of an old parlor organ. Originally, the
top must have been four feet wide, although by the time I
found it in a junk shop, a good portion was damaged or missing. But it was unusually pretty, and there appeared to be
enough left to make *something*—besides, for only four dollars,
how could I pass it up? So, bringing it home, I laid the organ
top on the basement floor in order to study and weigh its
possibilities. Then, with only a vague idea in mind, I began
to take it apart. (Though each piece of old furniture is different, you'll find the general construction similar in many
cases.)

First, I removed all the screws from the back and underside, marveling at the way this piece was built. It was so old
that the glue had long since let go, yet it was still held together by wooden dowels in some places, while in others the

precisely cut edges fit into corresponding grooves. It reminded me of a puzzle, and with a few taps of the hammer, it came apart like one. This made the reassembly easier, although I didn't attempt any actual rebuilding until after I'd tried out every possible arrangement and chosen the one that looked best—the old scientific method again.

Here and there, it was necessary for me to remove the wooden dowels or saw them off, but wherever possible, I used the original pegs. Surprisingly, there was more than enough material for one wall piece. (I'm saving the leftovers until I find just the right board to use as a back for a second project of similar design.) But the first—the one in the photograph— I put together with glue and small brads, tying heavy twine tightly around the whole thing in both directions to hold it until the glue was dry.

While assembling this piece, I found that a couple of the decorative ends, or knobs, were broken off, so I replaced these with metal finials from an old lighting fixture, as shown in Figure 1h. Actually, although I would have preferred wooden ones, the others (brass, and a trifle tarnished) didn't look too bad.

It was apparent that I'd also have to restore a missing knob on the lacy Victorian trim. But what to use? A search through my standby material turned up a dilapidated old rattan chair, and amid what remained of the once-extravagant rounds and curlicues on this ancient rocker, I spotted a small wooden knob exactly the right size.

While cutting it loose from the scrolled chairback, I took pains to leave intact a bit of the wooden shank, then used this to glue the knob into place. Although the knob was the same size as the original had been, it was made from a different kind of wood, so that the color contrasted sharply with the rest of the wall piece. But of course, with my system of trial and error, the watchword must always be cope, or there's bound to be a solution—all you have to do is find it.

This time it was easy. I decided to make the entire piece, including the added knob and metal finials, stark white, using a low-gloss spray paint. With so intricate a design, it covered better and took much less time than a brush would have. When it was finished, no one could ever have guessed which parts had been added.

Of course, someday I may yet run across the exact pieces I need (in walnut) to replace the off-color wooden knob and the metal finials, too. If I do find them, the white paint can then be stripped off, and the whole thing restored to its lovely natural walnut finish. In the meantime, my stark white wall piece provides an effective contrast with the red Victorian paper on my bathroom wall.

This waiting until you find special parts for the completion of a project works very well and can be carried even further.

For example, whenever a new idea strikes me, I can hardly wait to try it. But more often than not, after beginning to build, I find that there aren't enough parts or that they are not the right kind. Don't let that discourage you; just gather up all the parts you plan to build into your design, along with the picture or a rough sketch of what it is to be. A magazine clipping or little notation will do, so long as the *idea* is captured. This serves as a reminder not to use the parts for some other project until you've had a chance to look around for the missing pieces.

My plans for a second Victorian wall piece (if I can find the right type of wood) include finishing it in natural walnut.

Treadle Type of Sewing Machine

Only a short while back, every junkyard in the country was glutted with these machines. Many of them, standing outside and exposed to the weather, were already too far gone to be of any use. As with most things that nobody wants while they are plentiful and everyone covets once they're scarce, old-fashioned sewing machines may soon become true treasures and exceedingly hard to find.

At present there are still a number of antique machines about—in attics and basements, as well as secondhand shops—and their uses are multiple. The cast-iron legs are in moderate demand for dressing tables or plant stands. The drawers, especially those with a carved design on one side, make very decorative planter boxes. Those with a rounded end in front can be soaked in water to remove the glued-on curve. Or leave the curve as is, and use the two drawers, instead of one, to make a longer planter. For this, choose a right-hand drawer and a left one so that when the flat back ends are placed together, both side designs will face toward the front.

Some shops do not take time to salvage the rack or framework into which the drawers slide unless it is in perfect condition. This framework (Plate 14, Number 11) often consists of several pieces of wood fastened together, each one intriguingly grooved, beveled, or in half-round design. Such bits of molding make interesting trim, say on the flat top of a trunk or chest, as does the carved ornate wood from the front of the machine (unless the design includes lettering).

Sometimes, if a machine is in good shape, both the left- and right-hand racks can be salvaged along with the drawers. These can then be utilized as two separate units. Or you might have a top and bottom board cut large enough to en-

PLATE 17. Set of drawers in Swedish blue designed by Carol Simmons. Old sewing-machine drawers are incorporated into a carpenter-built framework, trimmed with fancy half-round molding. The drawers have been lined with wallpaper in a provincial print.

PLATE 18. Small chest of drawers by Carol Simmons. The chest consists of four sewing-machine drawers set into a carpenter-built frame work.

compass them both. Better still, get a carpenter or cabinet-maker to shorten the depth of the drawers a bit; then build them into a compact little set of four or six miniature drawers. These are stunning when painted and antiqued and used atop a desk or dressing table. (Plates 17 and 18.) Incidentally, the machine's beveled top can sometimes be used for the top or bottom board on such sets of drawers. Sets of six drawers can have a fairly substantial base added in order to gain a few inches of extra height, and then will make nice little end tables. (Plate 19).

The early treadle machine had a removable box that could be locked in place over the head of the machine. These boxes are found in a variety of styles. Some are rounded at the corners and veneered—almost contemporary in design and, to my way of thinking, not nearly so pretty as the plainer square-cornered ones—many of which are oak or walnut with interesting detail.

The wall piece in Plate 20 was made from such a box. It was first sawed in two (lengthwise) and half-mounted on a board cut to the same size. Small finishing nails, plus all-purpose glue, were used to fasten it to the board, which had been given a coat of walnut stain. A couple of holes were drilled in the backboard in order to hang it.

Wooden Bowls

For a change of pace, I'd like to tell you about a quaint old-fashioned type of candleholder. Since it reminds me of pictures in *Mother Goose's Nursery Rhymes,* I call it a Jack Be Nimble.

The basic element in its design is a wooden nut bowl, the kind often found in secondhand stores. Centers inside these

PLATE 19. Small end table built from old sewing-machine drawers. Designed by Margaret Paxton of Milwaukie, Oregon, the drawers are finished in antique red, have a carpenter-cut top added, as well as a deep base for extra height. Original molding from old machine is used on the sides. The potpourri jar and tree candelabrum were designed by the author.

PLATE 20. Wall pieces by the author. The one on the left is in natural walnut with brass trim. It was once a wooden cover for an old-fashioned sewing machine. The wall hanging is a fabric remnant ornamented with finials (see Figure 1) and brass jewelry.

bowls are usually raised an inch or two, and some have a small metal plate fastened to this raised platform, which can be either pried up or lifted off by removing a couple of screws. (Also, peel off any felt glued to the bottom of the bowl, using water or a scraper to remove stubborn areas.)

Next, drill a hole all the way through the center of the bowl (using a 7/16 bit).

The nut bowl has now become a base for your candlestick.

Select a lamp rod six or seven inches long and start to build, using the same basic method described in Chapter 4, with a single exception. Since the nut bowl is perfectly flat on the bottom, you will need to enlarge the center hole a bit at the point, with either the drill or a knife—just enough to recess the nut, thus allowing your candlestick to sit flat.

Now try different metal or wooden parts (or a combination of both) together on the rod till you achieve the most attractive result. You may want to start out, as I did, with a hollow metal part large enough to completely cover the raised platform, then to go on up from there. Follow as nearly as possible the general proportions of the Jack Be Nimble pictured in Plate 21. (Don't forget, you can assemble composite parts of similar shape.) When you have decided what pieces you want, string them on the rod, add a nut top and bottom, and tighten.

The handle goes on last. For this you will need a curlicue of metal (usually wrought iron) with a couple of holes in strategic spots for fastening it to your candlestick base. Nearly every piece of secondhand wrought iron has a few holes drilled in it here and there. By taking care to adapt and use already existing holes, I've never yet found it necessary to drill a hole in heavy metal or wrought iron (and, in fact, wouldn't know *how* to do it if I had to).

PLATE 21. Jack Be Nimble candlestick by the author. This quaint candlestick was made from a wooden nut bowl and an assortment of metal parts. The candlestick is dark-green, shown here with chartreuse berries and candle.

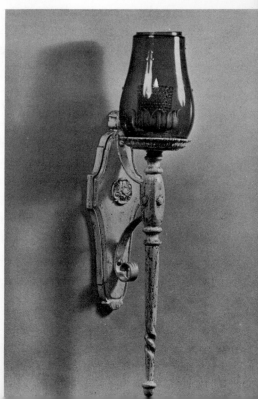

PLATE 22. Sconce by the author. Reconstructed from an old wall light, the sconce can be used with or without lantern chimney. The chimney is blue-green; the sconce white, antiqued in gold.

Incidentally, the attractive sconce in Plate 15 was also constructed without any drilling of metal. Existing holes in the wrought iron were used, along with some small screws, to fasten the arms to the half table leg.

As building material for decorative items, castoffs that are made of plastic have never appealed to me. However, this is not true of all manufactured materials. There are certain older pieces of Syrocowood, or composition wood—in particular, the smaller items such as boxes or ashtrays—that not only make attractive building pieces, but are quite sturdy and can be used in numerous ways. You will find in Plates 22 and 23 examples of two entirely different ways for using the same identical piece—first, as the base for a candleholder, then, upside down, as a middle building part in a lamp.

It is a simple matter to drill a hole in the center of such a piece, and by so doing, it immediately becomes an ornate part of anything in which you include it. Notice how rich the deep-carved design looks after being painted and antiqued. The one I've used as an illustration, in the candlestick and in the lamp, is just five and a half inches in diameter and originally held a glass ashtray (ashtrays with indentations to hold cigarettes or cigars are unlikely prospects, for obvious reasons). These small building parts are favorites of mine. They can also be found in square or oblong shapes, which are harder to use, since you won't often find a wood or metal piece the right shape to cover the center depression.

While our main interest is in castoffs or junk, be sure to keep an eye out for new products or man-made materials that can serve you as well. It is now possible to buy inexpensive, present-day versions of the beautiful, carved wood moldings and embossed plaster ornaments which lent so much charm to the houses of an earlier time.

PLATE 23. Lamp by the author. Junk shop finds, including a crock with a hole in the bottom and a metal bucket, were used in constructing this piece.

These are reproduced in a composition material that can be applied with a special type of adhesive, then painted to resemble stone, plaster, or wood. You will find these at building supply centers or in larger department stores.

Though it's true that discarded plastic articles do not adapt well, the interesting new method whereby colored glass is set into liquid plastic has now become quite a creative hobby in itself—one that might be worth exploring as a decorative aid in your transformation of junk.

Miscellaneous Odds and Ends of Wood

There are many fascinating bits of wood and equally as many ways they can be used. It would take an entire book to cover all of them, so we'll just touch lightly on a few before going on to the next chapter.

The fancy endpiece from a wooden curtain pole. This was just the thing for finishing off the bottom end of the table leg sconce in Plate 15.

Varnished wooden candlesticks. These are not usually hollow in the center, but they often have a good, though plain, base which can be removed. You may, of course, prefer to use the candlesticks as they are, perhaps in a group along with several others that are similar, either painting them different colors or all alike.

The middle pieces from old wooden floor lamps. Remember, you can saw a lanky wooden floor lamp apart wherever you want and intersperse the plainer wood sections with ornate metal pieces to liven up your design. Then, too, if small holes are drilled in the wooden parts, it's easy (with small screws) to attach metal flowers, wrought iron, or whatever else you wish. As these varied possibilities reveal, adaptability is one of the paramount virtues of wood.

6

The Wooden Candelabrum

I n this chapter we will take up multicupped candlesticks. Let's look at the wooden candelabrum shown in Plate 24. For those of you who have never used a saw or an electric drill, it might be wiser not to choose this as your first treasure-making venture, without the help of someone accustomed to such tools. However, if a candelabrum is your heart's desire, you needn't wait. There are several ways of building one that are not difficult even for a beginner. These are detailed in Chapter 9. In the meantime, keep an eye out for the kinds of pieces you'll want when you finally do build a wooden one.

For those who are ready to start on it right now, let's begin with the one in Plate 24 and trace its evolution. I had discovered an old-fashioned library table in a junk shop, and for some reason the curved section supporting its top reminded

PLATE 24. Large wooden candelabrum made by the author utilizes metal parts from old fixtures, odds and ends of wrought iron, portions of two tables, and pieces of metal jewelry.

me of a Swedish candelabrum I'd once seen. Here was the germ of an idea; once you have that, a design seems to develop almost of its own accord. The first step leads quite naturally to the next and to all the other nexts.

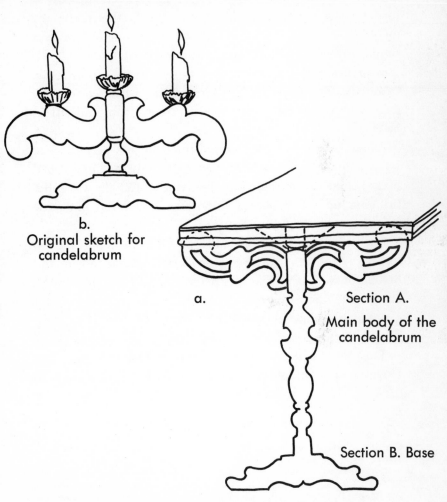

b.
Original sketch for
candelabrum

a.

Section A.

Main body of the
candelabrum

Section B. Base

FIGURE 6. Table leg used to build a candelabrum and author's pre-construction idea of how the finished piece (Plate 24) might look.

How to Make Something from Nothing

For example, in building this candelabrum, it seemed to me that the wide part at the bottom of the table leg should be about the right size to serve as a base. Why not, I reasoned, cut out the long middle part of the leg and put the curved top and the bottom (or base) together? At this point, my mental picture of how the finished piece might look was similar to the bottom drawing in Figure 6a.

A preliminary step was to remove the screws joining the battered table top to the leg. This left me with two separate sections: (A) the main body of the candelabrum and (B) its base.

As is common in most tables of this style and period, there was a hole right through the center of the base where it had been bolted to the table leg. The rest of the leg was solid, bringing up the problem of how to fasten top and base together.

I drilled a hole about one and a half inches deep in the top section (A). Next, turning this section upside down and bracing it in that position, I partially filled the hole with an epoxy glue* and inserted in it a threaded metal rod, about eight inches long, but smaller in diameter than a standard lamp rod. (Figure 7a.)

The glue was allowed to set overnight. Then, the next day, I strung a few middle parts onto the rod before joining it to the base. (Figure 7b and c.)

---

* This glue, sold under various brand names, can be bought in hardware, drug, grocery, department, or dime stores. It comes in two parts—one a resin, the other a catalyst—and you mix it yourself in whatever quantity you wish. Where strength is needed, epoxy not only holds like iron, but can give added bulk or thickness as well. One caution: Ignore the part of the directions that advise mixing it with the handy little applicator at the top of the tube. If you follow this procedure, you'll have glue clear to your elbows. Use a flexible old knife, instead, and wear gloves. Nail polish remover is fine for cleaning the knife and to take off any excess glue afterward. (Also see Chapter 11 for other types of epoxy, as well as more specific information on its use.)

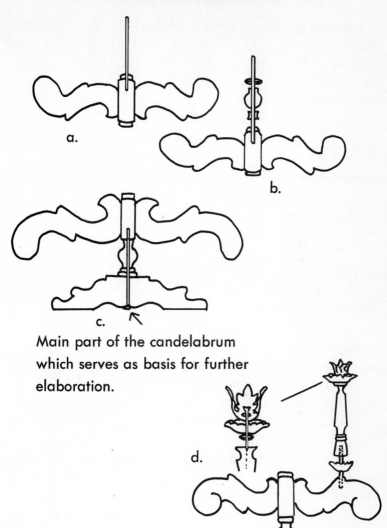

a.

b.

c.

Main part of the candelabrum which serves as basis for further elaboration.

d.

FIGURE 7. Step-by-step construction of the candelabrum in Plate 24, showing addition of table leg posts to improve design.

One reason this particular candelabrum is more time-consuming to build than most pieces is that the glue must dry thoroughly between each stage of the operation. While waiting, however, you'll have a chance to work on other things, as well as time to plot your next move.

Mine was immediately apparent once the base and top had been joined. The base looked fine and afforded enough support lengthwise, but it was inclined to tip backward or forward very easily. So, with ordinary glue, I fastened to the base two shaped pieces of wood. These served as braces—one centered in front, the other at center-back. A small screw was added in each case for extra strength.

I now had a sturdy framework on which any one of several different ideas could be elaborated. Had I stayed with my original plan (Figure 66), the project would have been almost complete. But being able to change one's mind is part of the fun, so why not experiment?

For effect, I tried all kinds of parts, including every candle cup* I could find. The table leg sections crowned with metal flower cups—often found on old wrought-iron ceiling fixtures —were my final choice, though for a time, the finished candelabrum had only three of these. The other two were added later.

The next problem, then, was how to join the three table leg sections to the curved main part of the candelabrum (Figure 7c). I drilled a hole, a little more than an inch deep, in the bottom end of each of the three legs, then followed nearly the same procedure as before, sinking a short metal

---

* A candle cup means anything that will hold a candle. For instance, the cup-shaped metal pieces (from an old ceiling light fixture), used here between the table leg sections and the main body of the candelabrum, make excellent candleholders as well. In fact, nearly any kind of part will do so long as it's a pleasing shape. If a candle can be set *in* or *on* it, a little florist's clay will assure its staying put.

rod, about two and one-half inches long, into each hole, which had already been lined with glue. You may prefer to use a wooden dowel instead of a rod. (Doweling, which comes in a wide range of sizes, is what the perch in your parakeet's cage is made of. It can be bought by the foot at lumberyards or woodworking shops; some dime stores and department stores carry it as well.)

I braced and tied the three table legs, bottom end up, until the glue had dried. Then I set about deciding where and how to fasten all three to the uppermost edge of the candelabrum (Figure 7d). Where the center leg was to go, I drilled a hole large enough to contain the rod, which was now firmly imbedded in the table leg.

Next, I marked off the positions the other two would take, and repeated the hole-drilling process. It was time now to glue all three into place—but first, I added a pretty cup-shaped metal piece underneath each leg. These served no particular purpose here, beyond contributing to the overall interest of the design.

Both the flower-shaped candleholders and the ornate flanges under them are metal. (I recently found forty-eight metal flowers in a single St. Vincent de Paul salvage store. [See Plate 14, Number 6.] They came from a church that had been razed in an urban renewal area.) Three of these were added to the tops of the wooden posts with slender two-inch screws as shown in the diagram of the table leg candlestick in Chapter 5.

Again, the candelabrum could now be considered finished and ready to paint. But to me, it still seemed a trifle stark, so I experimented with curlicues of wrought iron.

The first piece added was Part One, Figure 8a. It had a hole in it at a point (x), so that was where I joined it to the

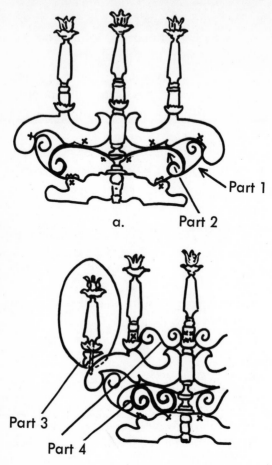

a.

Part 1

Part 2

Part 3

Part 4

FIGURE 8. a. Candelabrum when author first considered it finished shows wrought iron, parts one and two, in place. b. Shows later construction of two outside posts and addition of wrought-iron parts three and four.

wood with a small screw. The other end, which was cut straight across, fit firmly against the base. Even so, it ended too abruptly and looked chopped off. Some epoxy glue, plus a few metal leaves and flowers from old jewelry took care of this. At the same time I fastened Part Two to the wood at points (*x*) and again used epoxy and metal jewelry where it came into contact with the center post. This gave extra strength and solidarity, in addition to covering rough ends of the wrought iron.

I painted my candelabrum a soft turquoise antiqued in dark green and for a while was pleased with it. Then, eyeing my creation more critically one day, I decided it still needed *something*. But what?

I managed to find in my junk two more matching posts that were the same as the three on the candelabrum and tried holding them up to see if extra candleholders would improve the effect. The answer was obviously yes. And it was equally apparent that they'd have to be cut off shorter than the other three in order to follow the arc of the design.

Making a survey of my stockpile for the rest of the parts, I found I was stopped before I'd begun. I had one more flower cup, instead of two, and just one of the necessary metal parts that fit underneath.

The only solution was to set aside both the table leg posts and the metal parts, in hope of eventually finding the rest of the pieces. (I made a mental memo to be on the lookout in future treasure hunts for two small blocks of wood—properly shaped to glue onto the upper curve of the candelabrum— so that the two candleholders, if I ever found the necessary parts to assemble them, would sit level. See Figure 8b.)

It took almost a year, but I did find the missing elements, one or two at a time. This, by the way, is the essence of junking, the extra excitement that comes when you discover the one thing you've needed—and waited for—to finish some very special project.

By the time I got around to completing my candelabrum,

I'd also accumulated four more pieces of wrought iron that seemed to give it a little flair. The four round loops, as well as the metal flowers and leaves on the face of the candelabrum, were an afterthought, too. (I glued loops from light fixture chains into holes drilled in the wood. The round wooden decorations—directly above the outer pair of loops—were attached with ordinary glue.) The flowers and leaves were fastened on with tiny screws and epoxy.

There is a roughhewn look to the completed candelabrum which seems in keeping with this type of sturdy wood and wrought-iron construction.

By contrast, our second candelabrum, in Plate 5, has slender, delicate lines. Since there is less detail, it is also easier to put together. Except for minor variations, the same procedure was followed as with the first.

The diagram in Figure 9a outlines this candelabrum's structure and once more illustrates the method. But let's follow a few of the most important steps and touch on some additional ideas that will speed up construction of any wooden piece you build.

This candelabrum, like the other, started out as a small table—one that I'd thought of refinishing for my entrance hall. But it looked dated because of its height and was wobbly besides. So off came the top. Figure 9b shows where the table leg was cut to form the main part of the candelabrum.

Again, the first step was to drill a hole in the bottom of the curved section (A). But this time I used a standard 3/8-inch lamp rod so that I could add any base I wanted to later.

For me, it works best to drill a hole a little larger in diameter than the rod that is to go into it. This allows some leeway in adjusting the rod until it appears perfectly straight. (Remember to put some glue in first.) Then, if necessary,

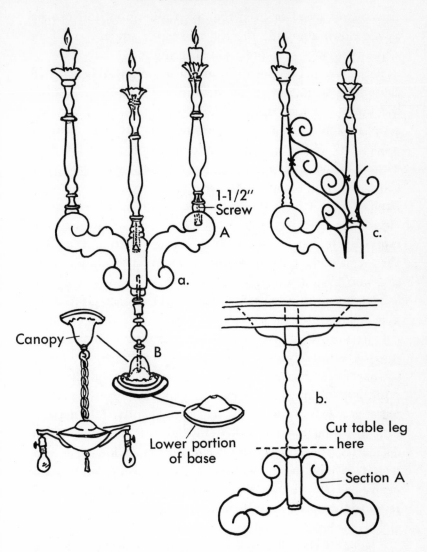

1-1/2"
Screw
A

a.

c.

Canopy

B

Lower portion
of base

b.

Cut table leg
here

Section A

FIGURE 9. a. Shows construction of candelabrum pictured in Plate 5. b. Sketch of table leg used for candelabrum in Plate 5. c. Suggested method of adding wrought iron to candelabrum.

tiny bits of wood or even crumpled aluminum foil can be poked down alongside the rod to keep it straight and firm while the epoxy sets—preferably overnight.

Perhaps you can borrow your husband's workbench, because here again, a vise is a definite help, both for drilling the holes and for applying the glue. Speaking of ways to simplify construction, I'm certain that any man with a moderately well-equipped workshop could do the whole project in half the time it took me. Nevertheless, here is a tip for those who don't happen to have either man or workshop handy. When I built the first candelabrum, which was quite large, the vise on my workbench proved inadequate, especially for some of the final gluing. Instead, I used a variety of objects as props (an old lamp with a heavy base, cast iron from a sewing machine, a wooden box), tying the candelabra to these so that it was in the proper position to glue and assemble the different parts.

Once the basic step is accomplished (gluing a threaded rod into the main body of the candelabrum), the design will begin to take form. Experiment with all sorts of candleholders, posts, and so on, but it's wise to plan the upper structure tentatively before adding the base permanently. This needn't stop you, though, from trying out different bases in order to decide how the finished candelabrum should look. For this reason, at least in this particular spot a threaded rod has a definite advantage over a wooden dowel in the construction. It not only allows room for adding extra middle parts, but also lets you select whatever base looks best.

The one I chose for this candelabrum is another example of a composite base. The bell-shaped piece, or canopy, was originally used to fasten an old light fixture to the ceiling. It could serve as a base by itself, but adding the bottom section (Figure 9a) made it look more balanced and gave the whole candelabrum better proportions. The two holes in the bell-shaped part where it had been attached to the ceiling were covered with brass paper fasteners (Chapter 11) *before* the lower portion of the base was added.

By the way, let us suppose that you've already glued the rod in your candelabrum, yet it's a little short to hold the base, plus all the middle pieces you'd like to use. If this happens, simply add a coupling and then another short length of rod.

It's curious how sometimes the least likely pieces work better than you expect. For example, the slender balustrade posts that were used here had been in my junk for ages. I got them through a newspaper ad (under "Miscellaneous"). The part that had caught my eye was "Wrecking large building, salvage for sale, all kinds."

The "building" turned out to be a big, square house—a very commonplace one. In fact, the only things I could see of any possible interest were eight or ten posts (painted an ugly buff color) that were built into the balustrade of a stair landing. Even these looked too spindly to be of much use. My junking instinct, however, got the best of me. When the wrecker asked what kind of material I was interested in, I pointed to the posts and asked, "How much do you want for those?"

"Well," he said, "what're they worth to you?"

I didn't particularly want them, but he was waiting for an answer. "A dollar and a quarter," I said, feeling like a penny ante operator.

"They're all yours, lady." He picked up a crowbar and in the time it took me to close my mouth, he'd ripped out not only the posts, but also the entire balustrade. He even carried the whole thing out to the car for me.

The minute I got home (trying to convince myself I'd struck a good bargain), I stripped a few of the posts to see what they looked like under that bilious paint. They were well-turned, nicely grained hardwood. But at the time I had no idea what they could be used for. I have since learned to wait until the right thing comes along.

The ends of these three posts that *made* my candelabrum were cut off, and with a coarse file, I smoothed any rough places. Whenever posts are sawed, especially small ones, the edges are apt to splinter, or tiny pieces may break off. Don't worry about it; the holes can be filled with wood putty (the dry kind you mix with water). This is a touch-up job and, like sanding, can be done just before you are ready to paint the completed project.

My balustrade posts, however, were so small in diameter that I substituted a 1 1/2-inch screw in place of a dowel or rod. (Figure 9a.)

Before you start to glue—even before you mix the epoxy—try positioning the posts on the candelabrum. You may need to file a few more rough or uneven areas. Keep in mind that when you put two pieces of wood together, either or both of them may be a trifle higher on one side. So turn them around until each compensates for the other's irregularities and they look straight from all angles.

Now, when they appear to be as true as you can get them, mark a spot at the bottom of each post and another directly below it on the candelabrum. (Use a dot of red nail polish, since the brush is featherlight and doesn't move anything out of position, whereas a pencil may.) When you're ready to glue the posts into place, just line up the red dots, and you can't miss.

Either before or after the candle cups are put on, wrought-iron curlicues can be attached, as shown in Figure 9c. Personally, I like the tall simplicity of this candelabrum better without them. But designs are as varied as each person's taste. For instance, I showed the finished piece to a friend, and she came up with a fine idea. She suggested tracing a pattern of the curved center section, then having a carpenter cut a number of them from unfinished wood with his electric saw. In that way, we could keep several pieces on hand. So we traced around half the design—which was all that was needed because the carpenter cut out two identical wooden sections—and doweled each one into a square center post. However, he did cut them a bit thicker than the table leg parts had been, so they required larger upright posts. As a result, while this second candelabrum is basically the same as the first, it looks quite different and has a charming Early American appearance.

But this wasn't the end of it. Another friend commented on my candelabrum, and I told her about our carpenter-cut middles. Immediately it brought to her mind an old table that had stood on her patio for a long time and that had a ruined top, but four nice, tall, slender legs.

Since her house is a far cry from Early American, she envisioned an entirely different candelabrum. Nevertheless, tracing around the same basic pattern, she took it to her neighborhood carpenter. He produced a curved section that was not so thick—more like the original. (He also assembled the entire thing for her after she'd explained her idea.)

But here is what intrigued me. I had thought the slim balustrade posts I'd used on my candelabrum were really quite tall. They weren't nearly as tall as the table legs that were added to my friend's (though, of course, the extra height was ideal in her spacious, high-ceilinged home). The whole effect—extreme and elongated—was unforeseeably striking. And as new as tomorrow.

With her usual flair for combining the old and the new, she chose to finish the candelabrum in white with antique gold. Then, for a final luxury touch, she added six long crystal prisms. Plate 6 illustrates this elegant contemporary version of the wooden candelabrum.

7

Wrought and Cast Iron

Aʟᴛʜᴏᴜɢʜ wrought iron is mentioned throughout the book I'd like to tell you about a few special things that can be done with it.

For a start, let's add wrought-iron arms and three matching candleholders to the table leg candlestick described in Chapter 5 and transform it into a candelabrum as shown in Plate 25.

Countless creations can be developed in this way, depending on the contour of the wrought iron. Now notice the candelabrum in Plate 26. Exactly the same kind of candlestick— the second one of a pair—was used here as a starting point, yet by adding dissimilar pieces of wrought iron and more ornate candle cups, it becomes an altogether different candelabrum.

PLATE 25. Triple candelabrum by the author. The candelabrum is a wooden table leg–candlestick, transformed by addition of wrought-iron arms. Shown here with milk-glass shades, this piece will also accommodate any number of other accessories, such as candles, small bowls, or vigil cups.

PLATE 26. Wall piece, box, and candelabrum by the author. The "before" picture of the wall piece is shown in Plate 3, Number 12. The hole in the center of this cast-iron stove top held a fancy metal finial (Number 21 in the same plate). A flat metal ornament was used in its place (see Plate 32). The hinged box has a hole drilled through the top and a metal ornament added to serve as a handle. The candelabrum is a wooden candlestick with wrought-iron arms and decoration attached.

Once again, the trick in working with any secondhand piece of wrought iron is to utilize the holes that are already in it. Use these for putting your creation together, and incorporate them into your design. This actually works better than you might imagine.

By the way, when pieces of wrought iron are stored in a box (as mine used to be), the curlicues become entangled, but I have found that by stringing a clothesline across one side of my basement workshop—two or three inches from the wall— my storage problem is solved. It's simple to hook curved ends of the wrought iron over this wire and certainly much easier to experiment with if all you have to do is unhook just one curlicue, rather than sort through a tangle of wrought iron.

A more complex version of the wrought-iron-on-wood theme is shown in Plate 27. In the center column of the candelabrum there are also some metal pieces (in addition to the base), such as a few parts just below where the wrought iron is attached. Above this point the column is composed of a series of wooden middles, and it is here that the iron curlicues are attached to the wood with small screws. The butterfly-shaped addition near the top is a single cast-iron part taken from the center of an old bridge lamp.

A candelabrum such as this one, assembled from odds and ends of wrought iron put together with tiny nuts and bolts plus epoxy, is another step-at-a-time production. It entails a fair amount of planning and more than a litle trial and error as well.

Though at first you may not want to attempt so involved a project, it is true that actually working with any material gives a better idea of what can or cannot be done with it.

Here's another thought: Occasionally, you'll create a rather special piece and perhaps give it away as a gift, only to wish

PLATE 27. Wrought-iron candelabrum by the author. Odds and ends and curlicues of wrought iron have been joined together with tiny nuts and bolts (see text). The candelabrum's central column includes several wooden parts. To these, the wrought iron is attached with small screws, dipped in epoxy.

later that you had one like it—or could remember how it was constructed. Duplicating a design is always difficult, but while trying to recall how I'd built the black candelabrum in Plate 27, I came up with an idea that has solved that problem. By tracing around one of these conglomerate designs, I can now have a metal shop reproduce the ironwork all in one piece (as was done for the centerpiece in Plate 28).

Keeping in mind that each arm *on the original centerpiece* had a lamp-rod-sized hole toward one end of the metal convolution, so that candle cup could be attached, and two smaller holes near the other end of each curlicue (for fastening the iron to a base), observe that the entire design was constructed from secondhand material. Even the wrought iron was put together by hand—the top curl which holds a candle cup was fastened to the lower curlicue with a thumbscrew and epoxy.

For the reproduced centerpiece in Plate 28, however, each wrought-iron arm was turned out as a single unit (minus the candle cup) by an ornamental ironwork shop. I could suggest one improvement, though. Have *three* holes drilled, instead of two, in your piece of iron where it is to join the center or base section. That way allows for a bit more leeway, since you can then use whichever two holes fit best for fastening the curlicue to the base and fill in the third.

Discovering a shortcut that accomplishes the same effect with less effort—even though sometimes it may cost a little more—is always immensely rewarding. I haven't explored the possibilities of the above procedure to any great extent, but you might investigate it further in case you're interested. (Note: Some metal shops do only large-scale commercial work for building contractors. Try to find one that specializes in smaller types of decorative designs.)

PLATE 28. Centerpiece built by the author is chartreuse, antiqued in umber. Milk-glass shades are used with accessories in soft tones of yellow and green. Though this centerpiece has a composite base, a single part, such as Number 3 in Plate 8, could be used instead.

PLATE 29. Small centerpiece made by the author for Merle Kirby. This is a simpler version of the centerpiece in Plate 2, requiring only two pieces of wrought iron. Bits of metal jewelry ornament the arms and cover unnecessary holes. The entire piece is painted white, antiqued in umber with a touch of green.

But getting back to the actual construction of this partially prefabricated centerpiece. In determining where the arms should be placed, it was essential to consider two things. First, they must be disposed properly for the later addition of candle cups, in order that the cups remain level. Second, as I've already mentioned, the contour of the base had to approximate the curve of the wrought iron where the two came together in order for the holes to be of any use. A composite base solved this problem. A lightweight easy-to-drill brass part was found—one that conformed to the curve of the wrought iron and made a good upper base section.

Positions of the iron curlicue's two holes were marked (with red nail polish) on this upper section, then drilled, and the iron joined to it with tiny thumbscrews and locknuts. As an extra precaution against the arms becoming loose or wobbly, epoxy was added to the underside, on top of, and around the locknuts. Once this had dried, and with the wrought iron firmly secured, it was an easy matter to assemble the other parts.

A simpler version of this centerpiece, requiring a single curlicue of wrought iron for each arm is shown in Plate 29. The compact lines of an oblong base allow it to be used where space is limited, such as on a shelf or a narrow mantel. You will find this general type of design unusually versatile to use in your home with different accessories. Gaslight shades offer an interesting change, but remember, you can achieve much the same effect with small bowls or vases of similar shape.

The somewhat fanciful piece in Plate 30 is another project that came about quite naturally, mainly because I'd uncovered some wrought-iron arms while scouting an urban renewal area and, in my eagerness to make the most of them,

PLATE 30. Wrought-iron decorator piece built by the author. The compote bowl is composed of two metal parts like the one in Plate 14, Number 10. Such parts are found on old-fashioned clothes racks. This particular piece is used by the author only at Christmastime and is adorned each year for the holidays with tall dripless candles and a festive arrangement of small Christmas tree balls and holly.

had experimented endlessly, meanwhile keeping an eye out for parts to go with them. Gradually, over quite a period of time and after several false starts, a design began to evolve.

If you have already rejected the idea of trying an elaborate piece because it looks too complicated, remember, it needn't be done all at once. When you are working on a complex production, concentrate on doing the first small step—perhaps just drilling several holes or gluing something into place. Then set your project aside, and come back to it later. There seems to be a creative psychology of sorts in plunging ahead at least to make a beginning. After that, take the relaxed approach, doing only as much as you feel like at the moment.

It's a fine idea to have several pieces in various stages of construction at once—some of them fairly simple. That way you won't be inclined to bog down. So long as you can see progress on any one of them, it will bring a sense of accomplishment to inspire you creatively. In any event, don't try to make an exact replica of this or any other piece, but improvise and let your imagination lead you where it will.

For the record, the candelabrum we've been talking about (Plate 30) was fashioned from a battered old iron ceiling fixture which was minus one of its five arms, but graceful, sweeping curves made up each of the four remaining ones. All four were utilized in this informally balanced arrangement. Of the two arms in the center, the one used below was flopped over so that its curves were reversed and leaned the other way—a matter of necessity since the holes in the wrought iron had to be aligned properly for candle cups. (The small extra curlicues of wrought iron were added later, with the use of epoxy.)

At the right-hand side, and the left, the other two arms were also placed at slight angles so as to distribute the holes evenly. (Again, the added bits of iron were not put in until later.)

The compote base was assembled using the lamp rod method. But in order to join it with the upper structure—the wrought-iron part—I resorted to some rather unorthodox construction: the open, shell-like bowl of the compote.

Remember those old wooden racks that were used many years ago for drying clothes—the kind that hung on the wall and had an oblong wooden back with slats opening out like a fan? If you will look at Number 10 in Plate 14, you'll see one of the metal parts from such a rack. This part was designed so that the slats radiated outward from it in a half circle, folding down flat against the wooden back when not in use. Two of these decorative pieces of lightweight cast iron (removed from a pair of racks) were joined with thumb-screws and small locknuts to form the compote bowl. And where they came together in the center, a gap was left—about 3/8 inch or perhaps a fraction more—just enough room to insert the lower ends of the wrought iron, thus clamping the entire upper structure into place. At the same time, the top end of the rod which extended upward from the preassembled base was held fast between them, and a nut screwed onto the top of the rod so it could not slip out.

Although that held the whole construction together quite well, it seemed slightly insecure. So I mixed up a cementlike tile-setting compound and, pouring it in, allowed this to run down into the compote portion and around the ends of the wrought iron (certainly not a procedure I'd recommend as a rule, but in this instance it has proved very satisfactory).

Since this candelabrum is somewhat flamboyant for every-day living room décor, I save it to spark my Christmas decorating and each year use a different arrangement in it. The tassels, incidentally, are brass, like the ones on the birdcage creation in Plate 69, but smaller. And they were attached with links from a metal chain bracelet. The center cluster of flowers also came from metal jewelry and was added to conceal joinings.

Now, about cast iron: Many of the bases you find will be made of iron, and a lot of the smaller parts, too. But let's consider ways of utilizing some of the less commonplace things you may run across on your junking trips.

The wall piece in Plate 31 was once a grille that covered a floor heating duct. This one was so unusual that I thought it pretty enough to hang on a wall with no further embellishment. (Two large holes, one at each end, where the grille had been fastened to the floor, were covered with decorative buttons.)

These old pieces of iron sometimes have small sections of the design cracked or broken out entirely. After mending two places in this particular grille and with it half-painted, I discovered another break still remained.

So study your design carefully. Then, wherever you intend to replace a missing curved section, take a piece of thin cardboard, and with a pair of nail scissors, cut out a slender curve the shape of the one that needs rebuilding—but a trifle longer to bridge the gap. Use the cardboard as backing for your epoxy, which is best added in two applications—just a rough outline over the cardboard first. When it's dry, use your palette knife (see Chapter 11) to build up a second layer. Let it dry and sand. The cardboard on the back can then be peeled off or painted over.

Note: A cast-iron piece similar to this one would be very striking painted flat black and centered on the lid of a low wooden chest, with other hardware on the chest painted

PLATE 31. Wall piece by the author. A cast-iron grille from a floor heating duct, found in a salvage store, has been redone in avocado green.

PLATE 32. Wall piece by the author. The cast-iron top of an old parlor heating stove is fastened to a carpenter-cut board with three-inch screws. This piece is white, antiqued heavily in umber, and it gives the appearance of being carved wood.

black to match. Or, of course, the whole thing—hardware, cast iron and all—would be equally effective done in a single color and antiqued.

In adapting an iron grille of plainer design for use as a wall piece, you might superimpose an old electrical wall bracket with the wiring removed. Attach the bracket to the grillwork, preferably in two places, with roundheaded screws, metal washers, and locknuts. Fasten them through open places in the cast iron, and use washers on both sides of the opening.

The baroque front of the wall piece in Plate 32 gives an appearance of carved wood. It is cast iron, however, and at one time may have been the pride of a housewife's heart as is graced the top of a parlor heating stove. (See Plate 3, Number 12.

A carpenter cut me a back for this from a piece of pine. But before the cast iron could be fastened to the wood (using two long screws), it was necessary to saw off—with a hacksaw—the little iron prong where it had once been hinged to the stove. It was his idea to leave a narrow grooved rim of wood showing around the curved edge of the cast iron, and I think it adds interest to the finished piece.

Obviously, iron—plain or fancy, wrought or cast—is particularly suited to present-day Spanish, Italian, and Mediterranean furniture, since many of these items incorporate iron as a part of their design.

Looking ahead, somewhat wistfully, I imagine the marvelous possibilities for reconstruction in our currently popular furnishings. What delightful castoffs such things will become—someday.

8

Wall Sconces

WITH very little effort you can transform old wall light fixtures into attractive sconces to hold vigil cups or candles. And there is no surer way than this to add a touch of glamor to your walls. Indeed, old gaslight shades, in all their delightful shapes and patterns, can be used to dress up your decorative wall brackets. When you set a vigil cup inside a shade and light the candle, the effect is absolutely enchanting. (I'll tell you how to adapt them a little later in this chapter.)

But what kinds of castoffs will you need to look for in building a wall piece? Don't limit your search to any particular category. Since old electrical wall fixtures are no longer in bountiful supply, it's encouraging to note they are by no means the only source of material from which you might assemble a sconce.

How to Make Something from Nothing

Witness the diversity of parts in the one in Plate 4. The back is cast iron (from an old stove) with a shaped piece of wood bolted to it—to form the top. A couple of drawer pulls are attached to the wood and serve as hangers. From a not-so-old ceiling fixture (one of the pseudo oil lamp variety designed to hold three small chimneys) came the three chunky middles for the candleholders. Each of these had a threaded rod soldered into one side—like the stem on a man's pipe. This was what first gave me the idea of using them on a sconce. They seemed ready-made for the purpose and needed only to be fastened onto a back.

Another advantage: There was a lamp-rod-sized hole in the center of all three parts, making it easy to run a rod through each, then to string on a few nicely shaped pieces and add a fancy loop at the bottom. (These loops are found on light fixture chains.)

No two designs will turn out just alike, nor are you apt to find exactly the same discards that were used here. But perhaps listing the assortment of material in this one will suggest an idea for using items in your own scrap pile that are similar.

In building this piece, stems of the three candleholders were anchored through holes in the scrolled cast iron. However, in order to support the stems and hold them securely, a metal washer was placed against the cast iron both front and back before a nut was screwed onto the stem and tightened.

As for the old electrical wall lights that you still find occasionally in secondhand stores or thrift shops, you can refurbish them as such if you simply remove the wiring, fill any holes, then paint and antique them. But they can be rebuilt, too. The arms and candleholders can be unscrewed from the backs and interchanged. Once you've dismantled some wall

PLATE 33. Accessories made by the author. The plant box is a sewing-machine drawer; the wall hanging, a printed linen towel with metal ornaments. The candle sconce is a reconstructed wall fixture, and the double-tiered compote consists mainly of two angel-food-cake pans.

lights, you'll realize how easy it is to reconstruct them to suit yourself.

For example, let's assume you are taken with a particular fixture, except that the arm is too rigidly straight for real grace. And the cup—this is shaped well, but it would hold only a candle, and you prefer using a vigil cup, which takes a larger holder. With these requirements in mind you can keep an eye out for a better-looking arm and a more suitable cup. (Sometimes the most unpromising castoffs will contain a single part that you need.) Or perhaps you can remove an arm from one fixture and the candle cup from still another. This is one way of being creative without really trying.

Before its transformation, the wall sconce in Plate 33 had but two candle arms. The sconce itself, being pot metal, was molded along with the arms into a single unit. In an effort to minimize its awkward, deer-antler look, two holes were drilled in the lightweight back, and a center arm was attached. Arms of this kind usually have their own tiny blunt-pointed screws, and these fit into holes with matching threads (8/32 inch) at the lower, broad end of the arm.

Sometimes discarded ceiling fixtures can be adapted as sconce backs, especially the oval type. (See Plate 34.) And once in a while you may find a round one that is unusually striking. The sconce in Plate 35 originally had a lightweight brass center soldered to its beautifully ornate outside rim. This I removed by melting the solder with a small propane torch. One of four existing holes was utilized to insert a brass arm taken from an old wall fixture similar to the one in Plate 3, Number 14. (Brass arms can also be bought new at lamp shops.) Another hole, at the top, was used to add a hanger loop at the back—the locknut securing it on the front side was then covered over with a bit of brass jewelry, while

PLATE 34. Wall sconce by the author. The sconce back was formerly a ceiling fixture like the one in Plate 8, Number 1. The back was buffed and polished; then a brass arm and gaslight shade were added.

PLATE 35. Polished brass sconce by the author. The intricately designed brass back was once a ceiling fixture with a plain brass center soldered to it. By melting the solder, the center section was removed. (See text.)

the two remaining holes were filled with large brass paper fasteners.

Now suppose you have an arm but no back to put it on. That's why it is such a good idea to save any interesting pieces of wood. (Or you might have a carpenter cut some for you, perhaps shaped and beveled around the edge.)

When it comes to making the most of *small* wall fixtures, unless they're in pairs or groups of three—or are especially attractive to begin with—you may prefer to dismantle them entirely and use the component parts to build really impressive sconces. This way you will gain a maximum of effect from your material.

For the table leg sconce in Plate 36, the arms and candleholders—the ones on either side and at the top—were taken from nondescript wall lights with flat steel backs that were so small I later discarded them.

The large wrought-iron arm in the center of the table leg came from an iron ceiling fixture which had five arms in all. (See Number 9 in Plate 14.) Though this would also have made a beautiful hanging piece (or even a chandelier if it had been rewired), by taking it apart the arms could be used for more than one decorative creation.

Not every table leg is suitable as a back for a sconce—at least not without being cut in two (lengthwise). The reason this one adapts so well is that it has two squared sections allowing it to fit flat against the wall.

It's best to determine first, before the arms are attached, how you intend to hang a sconce. You might improvise with small bits of metal from your junk, or there are excellent little hangers on the market (intended for wooden plaques or picture frames). You can buy them at dime or hardware

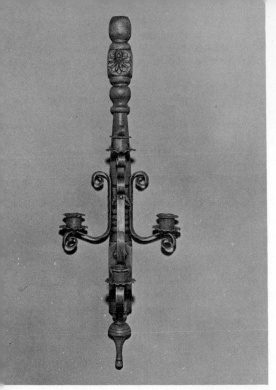

PLATE 36. Wall sconce by the author. The sconce is constructed from the table leg shown in Plate 3, Number 7. It is finished off at the bottom with the wooden end of a curtain pole and is painted chartreuse, antiqued in black.

PLATE 37. Wall sconce by the author. Made from half a wooden table leg, its decorative hanger is a loop taken from a fixture chain.

stores, and they come complete with nails or screws for fastening them to the wood.

One of the most efficient is a small oblong metal strap that hugs the back of a sconce and has a notched edge that's just right for gripping the nailhead. In using this type, fasten one on the back of the upper squared section of your table leg and another on the lower square. Although these hangers protrude only a fraction of an inch, a sconce looks better hanging perfectly straight. Better still, to fasten the sconce absolutely flush with the wall, chisel out a small area at the back of the leg and set the hanger in it.

Another type of hanger found at the dime store has cleats that can be pounded into the table leg back, leaving a small loop exposed at the top to hang over a nail. If your table leg is fairly heavy, you may need to reinforce these cleats with an added nail or a tiny screw. When used on a whole table leg, such as the one we're talking about, set the hanger in the top squared section with the loop extending upward beyond the square. On a half leg, place it so the loop shows above the top of the sconce.

Incidentally, for a sconce made from a half table leg, you can use a more decorative hanger such as an ornamental loop taken from a fixture chain. These loops are available wherever lamp parts are sold, but there will probably be some in your secondhand material, too. Choose one that's fairly ornate. To attach it, first rout out an area at the back of your table leg. This should be deep enough to recess the shank end so that it will be flush with the back of your sconce, allowing the decorative portion of the loop to extend far enough upward to show. (Plate 37.) Use a generous amount of epoxy to secure the loop in its little niche, and let it stand overnight to harden. Though you may expend more effort installing a hanger of this type, it will add flair and interest to your finished sconce.

For a decorative hanger that is simpler to install, you can buy at variety and hardware stores a charming little loop that comes ready-made to screw into the top of your wall piece. These are available in several sizes and styles, including a rope twist which antiques beautifully. This type of hanger is altogether satisfactory, except for very heavy wall pieces.

In selecting wrought-iron arms for a sconce, there must be a hole in the metal wherever you intend to put a candle-holder. Sometimes this hole will be large enough to hold a standard-sized lamp rod (or else a nozzle—see Figure 1d). Or it may be so very small you will find it necessary to fasten the candle cup to the iron with a tiny nut and bolt.

For the wall sconce in Plate 36, attaching the cups was not difficult because the metal arms, having been previously wired as a wall fixture, were complete with a threaded nozzle. (To attach a candle cup where a nozzle is used, simply screw a nut onto the nozzle end, and if the nozzle threads aren't long enough, add a coupling, more lamp rod, then the nut.) Also, take pains to arrange the wrought iron on the table leg so that your candle cups will remain comparatively level and not be tilted at a rakish angle.

Now for that extra bit of glamor I mentioned earlier. Here is how you can adapt your sconces to accommodate gaslight shades or small bowls in which candles may be burned.

As an example, let's say that you have a small plain single-arm sconce—admittedly something less than a conversation piece. What better way to dress it up than with the shimmer and sparkle of glass? Search through your stockpile for a part the right size to hold the bottom rim of a shade. Occasionally, you may find a shade holder complete with its little holder

screws to grip the shade. (See Number 7, Plate 14.) Reproductions of these are stocked in hardware or electrical
departments and priced very inexpensively.

In addition, you will need a coupling, and these are found
on almost any kind of castoff lighting fixture. (Or buy new
ones the right size for a lamp rod.) Couplings are practically
a must on your list of necessary material—screwed onto the
nozzle end of a sconce arm, they facilitate adding extra inches
of rod.

Since a shade holder has a large center hole, you'll want to
insert a large washer or a semiflat metal part of some kind
first, underneath the shade holder. This platelet will then
furnish a resting place for both holder and shade. The same
procedure is equally viable for any part you may have selected
instead of a shade holder (to set your shade on), at least if the
part has a center hole that is larger in diameter—for example,
one of those embossed, slightly cupped parts that was used to
encircle a light socket (Chapter 3). This wider type of flange
is more satisfactory if you intend leaving a gaslight shade on
your sconce permanently. You can then build a cup or platform inside the shade on which to set a vigil cup or candle.
To install a shade in this manner, choose a small cup-shaped
part that will snug down firmly *inside* your shade and *onto
the coupled extension of lamp rod*. Add a nut, and tighten
gently.

If you plan to burn a candle (without a vigil holder), it
won't matter at all that there's a bit of rod left over. You can
utilize this to impale the candle and hold it in place. My only
objection is the buildup of wax which must be removed after
each use.

When placing a vigil cup inside a shade, avoid contact of
glass against glass. Florist's clay is one solution, or perhaps

even a small jar lid—anything that will hold the cup up and away from the glass shade. My favorite part, however, for this purpose is the lower portion, or cap, of a light socket. Since it is threaded, the cap can be screwed onto the rod and in some instances will take the place of a nut. These may be left just as they are or filled with tile cement and camouflaged with a bit of chain. Note: Some are smaller in diameter than others, so check to see which size is best suited to a particular shade.

The wall bracket in Plate 22 was constructed in much the same way except that it features a blue-green lantern chimney (also set on a light fixture flange). This sconce is also decorative without the chimney, since it has a metal flower inside to hold either a candle or a vigil cup. You will find this sort of piece a pleasure to own, since it is highly effective added to a grouping of pictures and plaques in different shapes and sizes. More intriguing still is the play of light and shadow when a burning candle casts its glow over the entire arrangement.

9
Compotes and Candelabra

CERTAINLY among the most versatile of decorator items, and perhaps the most fun of all to build, are compotes and candelabra—ranging from unpretentious footed bowls and simple candelabra to elaborate creations containing features of both.

An epergne type of compote is pictured in Plate 38. Though its size is not apparent in the photograph, this is quite a large piece and an excellent one for holiday décor. Excluding the two bowls, which are metal, it is made entirely of wood put together with dowels.

Let's take another look at the compote bowl and the over-size candleholder. Notice how the sharply flared lines of the two bowls lend a sense of unity to the design. Yet each bowl was little more than a rim to begin with—just as you would

PLATE 38. This large epergne by Carol Simmons is constructed of wood, except for the two metal pans, and antiqued white.

build up a composite base or middle, single parts can be joined together to form a bowl. To make the bottom section of the larger bowl, a deep spun-aluminum lid with a center hole drilled in it was used (upside down). Underneath the smaller bowl, or candleholder, a metal part from an old ceiling light was added.

The compote candelabrum in Plate 39 derived its inspiration from the part which forms its compote bowl. This part, also taken from a ceiling fixture and made of embossed brass, was really quite pretty and ornate, except that it had (unfortunately, I thought) *five* lamp-rod-sized holes spaced at intervals around its flat inner edge. This seemed a few too many to cope with, though as usual, the problem solved itself with a little experimentation.

I fastened odd lengths of lamp rod in the holes, then strung wooden spindles on them (found on a broken Early American floor lamp), along with an assortment of other small parts. In order to stagger the heights of the candleholders, extra pieces were added to bottoms of taller ones—so all the tops would appear to be constructed the same.

In converting pans or light fixture parts into compote bowls, you're apt to encounter a number of holes, apparently in all the wrong places. Very seldom are these beyond saving, because there are numerous ways to camouflage them, which we will go into in some detail later. The point is, however, that holes can often be an asset.

The compote in Plate 40 is another instance in which a design resulted from an abundant supply of leftover holes. One day, while trying to determine what I could make from the remaining portion of an ugly old ceiling light—one with a multitude of holes—I hit on the idea of utilizing them to attach pieces of wrought iron and small brass curlicues. This

PLATE 39. Swedish blue compote-candelabrum by the author. Each spindle is constructed of several small parts. Staggered heights of spindles were achieved by adding extra parts to bottoms of the taller spindles.

PLATE 40. Compote and shadow box by the author. There are three wrought-iron curlicues attached to the compote (see text). Each piece of iron curves up over the outside rim and down inside the bowl to the center. Additional small curlicues were added as ornamentation, along with the metal tassels. The shadow box once housed a clock.

did wonders for the bowl, giving it a new look that suggested the Spanish or Mediterranean.

Hunting through my discards for a suitable base, I came across the spindly-looking table lamp in Plate 8, Number 10. As you can see, it has an attractive base, and to me it seemed just right for this piece. I sprayed the finished compote a flat black. Of course, black will also make a fine undercoating, should I decide later to paint over it and antique.

You are certain to buy an occasional secondhand item that proves difficult to transform. You will also acquire some that are uncommonly pretty. And these you will want to use as effectively as possible. Often, the best way to dramatize such a favorite is to make it the focal point of a very plain, uncomplicated piece.

Simple lines draw attention to a richness of design in the compote basin in Plate 41. Inside the basin is a raised semi-flat plate to hold a candle, though it is built up only a little way, so that it won't show should the candle be omitted.

The base of this piece is metal, with cement poured in the bottom to provide ballast for the larger, heavier top. The middle portion is a series of wooden parts. And the fancy compote bowl? It was once the base of a cast iron floor lamp (turned upside down). The bottom section of this simulated bowl is a metal part, which also serves to cover a good-size opening in the center. (In its former existence as a floor lamp base there had been at this point a flat piece of marble.)

The centerpiece was antiqued in blue, over white. If the clean Dutch look of blue and white appeals to you, here is another color note: There is a sunny charm in this particular shade of blue when it is complemented by a yellow candle and blue and yellow flowers—not a bright yellow, but a soft,

PLATE 41. Compote by the author is white, antiqued in blue. The bowl of the compote is the metal base from a floor lamp turned upside down.

beigy one, deepening to gold about the tone of yellow ocher (as in a tube of oil paint).

The versatile tree candelabrum (Plates 42 and 19) will hold either vigil cups or candles and is great fun to decorate for special occasions. Although moderately tall, it lends itself well to compact arrangements, for instance, close to a wall or on a window ledge.

Having built a number of these, each, of course, a bit different, I've found it takes awhile to accumulate enough material. So reserve a box especially for tree candelabrum parts. These include all sorts of small middles and fill-in pieces, plus any arms (threaded at both ends) that are shaped just so—with the required straight or semistraight stem curving upward at the end. (See Plate 8, Numbers 6 and 11.)

Such arms, which are usually too awkward and straight to use on a sconce anyway, are often found on rather tinny-looking pinup lights. The arms will probably be all that is salvageable, so don't pay too dearly for them.

For each candelabrum you will also need three special parts—these are used at the center of the tree, one at each point where the arms branch out. They are threaded inside and similar to a coupling, but with a four-way hole—one opening extends directly through the center, but they are also tapped and threaded so an arm can be screwed into each side. You'll be surprised how many of these will show up in your secondhand material. So far I've never needed to buy a new one, though, of course, you can. Such a piece is called a brass arm end. (Some are tapped on only one side.)

Then there are larger parts called cluster bodies which have as many as three, four, or five threaded side holes. Others —the kind you'll be looking for—have just two holes, one on each side. (Plate 8, Number 6.) These, if fairly small,

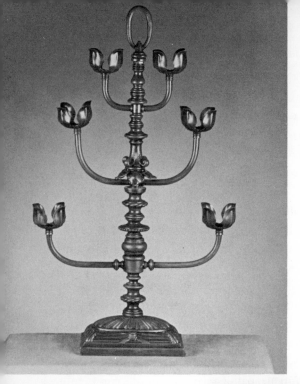

PLATE 42. Espaliered eighteen-inch tree candelabrum with composite base made by the author for Merle Kirby. It was assembled from many small secondhand parts. Particularly suited to compact arrangements, this espaliered design is excellent for small rooms where space is a problem (see Plates 64, 65, and 19).

PLATE 43. Antiqued gilt compote by the author. Though this compote's built-up base is metal, there are several wooden parts in its center column. The ornate candle arms came from a floor lamp; the bowl is a pan lid; and the metal flowers were found among odds and ends in an antique store.

will do for a tree candelabrum. (Note: On floor lamps, the cluster bodies often have permanently attached arms which cannot be unscrewed and, therefore, work better for creating other types of candelabra.)

Once you've acquired the three necessary center parts and enough arms, the rest of the pieces are no problem. Of course, you may prefer to construct a double- instead of a triple-branched tree or to add a loop at the top rather than a candle-holder—or to vary the design in any way you choose.

But here is how you start: Put together your graduated sizes of arm branches. Remember, the arms must be threaded at both ends so that each can be screwed into the side hole of an arm end or cluster body, and a candle cup added to the other end. (Don't screw the arms in far enough to interfere later with the center rod.) Now lay out all three pairs of arms on the floor, and determine approximately how far apart they must be on the rod in order to form an espaliered tree.

Choose a base, not a very large one—either round or oblong will do nicely for this type of piece. If possible, use a single threaded lamp rod which goes all the way to the top for the backbone of your tree. Should you encounter difficulty in getting the arm ends or cluster bodies situated right on this rod, use short lengths of rod as an alternate, and assemble your tree in sections, with the centralized arm ends or cluster bodies serving to couple one section to the next. Add a pro-portionate number of middle pieces between each arm branch.

Here is another point that may prove helpful: The lower tree branches can be extended outward if necessary by adding a bit more lamp rod in each side hole of the central cluster body and then stringing on a few small middles before the arm is screwed into place.

In this way, you can also utilize arms that have more curve or ones of equal length. For example, if you have only four matching arms and they're all the same size, you can still

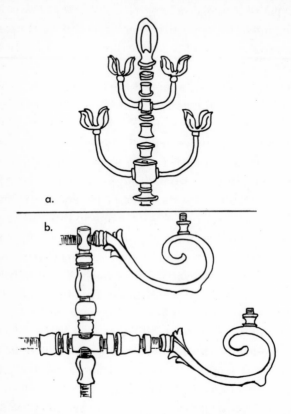

FIGURE 10. a. How to assemble center column of tree candelabrum (see Plates 42 and 64). b. How to build a tree candelabrum using arms of same size (see text).

build a two-branch tree candelabrum as shown in Figure 10b —that is, if they are shaped similarly to those in the diagram.

In building a more conventional candelabrum, any kind of old light fixture having multiple arms will provide you with an excellent start. But one of the simplest parts to adapt is a three-arm cluster from the top of a floor lamp (Plate 3, Numbers 8 and 9; also Plate 8, Number 8). A similar part, with the electric wiring, sockets, and simulated cardboard candles removed, was transformed into the compote candelabrum in Plate 43. Incidentally, this particular floor lamp happened to be an exception to the rule; it had a cast-brass cluster body, threaded on three sides so that the arms were not permanently affixed but could have been removed, had I decided to use them separately. And I did consider this possibility, since they would have been beautiful for a multiple-arm wall piece or, polished and used separately, would have provided the arms for three stunning brass sconces.

For use on this compote candelabrum, however, the hexagon-shaped cluster body with its three ornate arms was strung on the lamp rod as a single unit.

Here is a clue to improve almost any candelabrum's design. Your creation will appear more balanced if it is a trifle taller in the center. Allow enough length in your lamp rod; then put on a few extra middle pieces to build it up to the desired height.

The same principle applies when a loop handle is used instead of a center candleholder—as on the simple little candelabrum in Plate 44 (made from a different type of floor lamp). Here, the center column is even higher, reaching well above the three cups and having several middle parts added to it before the top loop is screwed onto the rod. How much more effective this is than it would have been had the loop been nestled down in the center at the same level as the candle cups.

There is still another type of floor lamp that I'm always happy to find. It has a U-shaped top which is very adaptable.

PLATE 44. Candelabrum in dark green by the author. The candle arms came from a small cast-iron floor lamp and were added as a single unit. The large finial at the top was taken from an old ceiling light.

PLATE 45. Small candelabra by the author. Both are made from floor lamp tops. A "before" picture of the one on the right can be seen in Plate 8, Number 4. The contemporary candelabrum in Plate 7 was made from an identical floor lamp.

(The small candelabrum on the left in Plate 45 was made from such a top.) These are found in various designs. Some, like the one in Plate 8, Number 4, are not very pretty, yet even so unpromising a lamp has potential. As I mentioned in Chapter 3, the ornate candelabrum on the right in Plate 45 is a by-product of this particular castoff, and so is the contemporary piece in Plate 7. For the modern design, after wiring and sockets were removed, the floor lamp top was not altered except for a change of candle cups, and here again, Figure 2 shows how this was accomplished. Since together the two floor lamps yielded four matching cups, I elected to save these for some future project which might require that many.

In building the more elaborate of the two pieces (see Plate 45, right side), the floor lamp top was first placed in a vise; then a hacksaw was used to remove the design's central jagged portion. This was fairly easy, since it required sawing through only two narrow points on each side. The fancy middle section of my candelabrum, including the cluster of small metal flowers, I found centered on another old floor lamp, and the entire ornament was removed in one piece. (As these flowers had been *welded* to the lamp's central pipe, a hacksaw was used above and below the floral design, removing pipe and all—the pipe being large enough in diameter to run a lamp rod through its center.) The whole thing fitted so perfectly, replacing the part I'd sawed out, that immediately my candelabrum began to shape up. The next logical step was to add a few small middle parts to this central stem, above the flowers, building it up a fraction taller than the sides to ensure a rounded graceful line.

Plate 3, Number 10 shows an old ceiling fixture the way it appeared when found in a salvage store. Pictured in Plate

PLATE 46. Compote, screen, and candlestick made by Carol Simmons. The compote was made from part of a ceiling fixture exactly like Number 10 in Plate 3. It is finished in antique white. The screen is oak skirting from an old square dining table. The candlestick is olive green.

PLATE 47. Centerpiece by the author. The starting point for this design was the pot metal castoff in Plate 3, Number 10.

PLATE 48. Wooden epergne by Carol Simmons. This piece is built entirely of wood. Both the candleholder and the bowl are wooden salad bowls from a salvage store.

46 is the same fixture rebuilt into a table centerpiece. A lamp-rod-sized hole was drilled in the center of the pot metal bowl, and one small wooden part was added underneath, as a middle. The metal canopy which formerly held the fixture against the ceiling was turned upside down to become a base.

The socket holes were filled in by a simple method which may appeal to some of you since it requires practically nothing in the line of material and can be applied to any such castoff in cases where socket holders are an integral part of the fixture itself. When you open small juice cans, therefore, save the flat tin tops. One of these lids set into a socket hole and secured with epoxy will form a holder into which a vigil cup fits perfectly.

A second centerpiece (Plate 47) was reconstructed from exactly the same kind of fixture, using a square base and a different procedure for the candleholders. Here the light socket holes were filled in by treating them as you would any other part that has a large center opening—reducing it first to lamp rod size. So find two washers or metal rings with that size center hole, and make sure they are a fraction larger than the socket's bottom opening. Place one of them above, one below, with a short lamp rod through both center holes. (Add a nut to the rod's top end.) Next, the small middles are strung on underneath with a finial screwed onto the bottom end of the rod to hold them there. Last, tighten the top nut (down inside the socket).

The quaint little epergne in Plate 48 looks as if it belonged in a cozy pine-paneled room. The entire piece, including the two salad bowls and square base, is made of wood. It was constructed with dowels, plus two long slender screws for attaching the candle bowl and base. Since secondhand wooden parts seldom match in color, this one was painted a

PLATE 49. Polished brass is used as a base for gaslight shades in this epergne made by the author.

warm brown and antiqued to retain its natural wood appearance.

A shade holder, like the ones discussed in Chapter 8, holds the smaller of two gaslight shades in the brass epergne in Plate 49. And a larger holder (also with screws to grip the shade) is built into the epergne at a lower level. As I said earlier, the key to adapting these parts to your building is to reduce the overlarge center opening by the addition of seating rings, check rings, or washers directly above and below the shade holder. Or, as in the case of the larger holder, cover the center opening with a part of some sort that is also large enough to serve as a support underneath the shade holder. Place another part equally large in diameter above and inside, thus converting the hole to lamp rod size. Then clamp the holder firmly between the two parts before anything more is added above.

A rather ordinary glass shade from a center-of-the-room ceiling light manages to fool the eye and become a top for the tall brass compote in Plate 34. Masquerading as an elegant frosted glass bowl, it has a fancy brass chimney holder set down inside, permanently affixed as part of the compote, which serves to hold a generous-sized candle or to anchor an arrangement of fruit or flowers when a candle is not used.

A round platelike part with five decorative brass extensions is shown in Plate 14, Number 2. Such fixtures or parts of them are fairly common, though you'll find that some have two, three, four, or six arms, instead of five, as shown here. Those with two or three brackets make good compote bowls with the fancy extensions left where they are and utilized as arms to support candle cups. For example, the centerpiece in Plate 50 is constructed from a small two-bracket fixture. Originally, light sockets dangled from chains at the end of

PLATE 50. Centerpiece by the author. It is constructed from a small two-bracket ceiling fixture. The two arms have been retained to form candleholders.

these brass extensions. At this point there were threaded holes, making it possible to add short lengths of lamp rod for attaching candle cups, as well as the metal tassels underneath.

There are endless styles and variations of compotes and candelabra for you to try. But whatever you build or where-ever you use it, don't underrate the magic of candlelight. For most of us it brings thoughts of a cozy hearth, festive occasions and enjoyable food with congenial friends. So set the scene. In that last moment before your guests arrive, light the candles. They'll bring a lift to the spirit and warmth to your home.

Part III

ON THE PRACTICAL SIDE

IO

Painting, Gilding, Antiquing

Exciting things are being done with color today, but before we go into that, let's talk about the preliminary steps.

Preparation for Painting

To go back a bit, you'll find it helpful if the parts you've chosen for your building have been previously scrubbed, sanded, or stripped. This is easier done beforehand than after your candlestick or centerpiece is already assembled—with the exception of occasional rough spots that require light sanding.

Stripping, however, is not necessary unless the paint is excessively chipped and patchy. For one thing, wood that has

How to Make Something from Nothing

been thoroughly stripped (particularly oak, if it is rather old) tends to be more porous and, therefore, harder to repaint than wood that still has some finish.

Metal, too, can sometimes prove more difficult stripped than not. For instance, pot metal often has an undercoat of black paint that may turn sooty and is hard to get rid of.

The following are methods which can be employed when paint must be removed:

Stripping Paint or Varnish

PARTIAL STRIPPING

1. For small spindles or middles of wood that have a coat of high gloss paint or shiny varnish, dampen a small cloth with nail polish remover, and wipe over them a few times, then once again with paint thinner. This takes only a few minutes, but it cuts the gloss and leaves the wood ready for painting.

2. Liquid sandpaper, which comes in cans, works much the same way, though not so fast, and is better on large pieces.

STRIPPING THOROUGHLY

1. Almost anything made of wood or metal, either large or small, can be commercially steam-cleaned.

2. If you prefer to do it yourself, use water-soluble paint remover (a liquid or jellylike solution that can be washed off with cold water). This is more useful on larger pieces or furniture. Ask your dealer to suggest a good product.

3. Alternates are lye, sal soda, or trisodium phosphate dissolved in *hot* water. Sal soda is slower but less caustic to work with, so resort to lye only when in a great hurry. Trisodium

is also milder but is unusually efficient for stripping heavily varnished pieces. In using any of these three substances, the following procedure is recommended:

Select the items you intend to strip—not too many at a time—and partially fill a good-size enamelware pan with water. (Reserve a canning kettle for this purpose.) Heat the water to the boiling point; carry the pan outdoors; then drop in the pieces to be stripped, plus approximately a cupful or more of either sal soda or trisodium—less if you're using lye. It is never advisable to add these caustics to boiling water indoors because of steam. Also, the solution is apt to bubble over the top of the pan. (A good place to do this is in a graveled area or cement driveway, where it can be hosed off afterward.) Avoid breathing the fumes. You can allow the pieces to soak, waiting till after the water has cooled to empty the pan; then remove the items and rinse them off.

Painting

A base coat or metal primer is applied, then your satin-finish color. (Either flat or high-gloss paint can be used if a coat of satin or low-gloss varnish is put over it and allowed to dry thoroughly *before antiquing*.) Incidentally, I have occasionally bought semigloss paint (custom-mixed) that was so dull I found it necessary to cover it with a coat of varnish before antiquing.

Another point to remember: Red mahogany varnish is very persistent, and even after stripping, it will sometimes "bleed" through several coats of new paint. So seal it with satin varnish first, before you paint.

The brightest colors antique best. Choose one much brighter than you intend the finished piece to be, since a color, once antiqued, will be less intense and have a softer, richer look. Most paint stores will custom-mix any color if you bring in a sample. They can even match a piece of fabric.

Despite the present emphasis on antiquing, there are occasional pieces that may be just as effective painted stark white. This would, of course, depend on how and where you plan to use them. (See Plates 30 and 15.) Flat black, too, is most appropriate for a dramatic piece with a Spanish flavor, such as the one in Plate 27.

Spray Painting

1. When you're in a rush, it may help speed things along to spray on a flat primer coat, then to use a brush to apply the satin coat—brush marks, as a rule, add charm to antiqued pieces.

2. When it comes to gold (though some decorative painters favor the brush-on variety), I prefer a spray paint.

3. If you use a spray type, be sure the can is kept at at least 70° F. Cold paint clogs and will not spray efficiently.

4. After you're through spraying, tip the can upside down and spray once more to clear the nozzle. As a further precaution, remove the nozzle and drop it into a small jar of thinner until the next spray job.

5. Don't hold the can too close to an object you are spraying, or the paint will bubble.

Antiquing Formula

The basic mixture consists of *equal parts of oil paint and paint thinner*—start with a tablespoon (or two) of each. Burnt umber is the color you'll probably use most often when antiquing. But there are all sorts of interesting color combinations, a few of which are listed in this chapter.

Oil paint will vary greatly in color and texture. To illustrate, one well-known brand of burnt umber comes in a warm brown, is quite moist, and easy to mix. Another equally famous brand is drier and produces a cooler, darker tone. However, it's all a matter of preference.

When it comes to mixing your antiquing formula, an old tableknife or a spoon will do, but for true efficiency you can't beat an inexpensive, flexible palette knife (artist's supply or stationery stores). I like the straight kind best, but this, too, is open to choice.

Antiquing Method

The best way to get the feel of antiquing is to do some. Use a small paintbrush to cover your creation thoroughly with the antiquing mixture. Pick up with the tip of your brush any puddles that may form in concave areas. When every curve and crevice have been coated, let the piece dry for five or ten minutes, till the shine begins to disappear. Now start rubbing with a lintless rag (such as a silk or rayon scarf), and wipe off the excess antiquing. Exert a bit more pressure here, a trifle less there, to create highlights and darker shading. Pat gently to blend or soften, but try to avoid working and reworking any area after it is reasonably smooth.

Finger marks can spoil an otherwise perfect antiquing job, so once you've finished, do not handle till it is dry (overnight).

Your individual taste will dictate whether you antique heavily or with a light hand. Though I am partial to dark antiquing, I have a tendency to get carried away and rub off too much.

Antiquing Tips

1. Store any leftover mixture in small covered jars, and label the color.
2. An emulsified or cream hand-cleaning agent—one that can be used with or without water—is surprisingly efficient for paint removal on arms or hands. (Gloves are too cumbersome to wear while antiquing.)
3. When doing a large piece such as the table centerpiece in Plate 51, you may prefer to antique it in two stages. First, do the base and center pedestal up to the arms. Then, when that section is dry—or even after its final coat of varnish—wrap the finished portion in plastic, and antique the arms, top bowl, and candle cups.

A Few Attractive Color Combinations

VERMILION

1. Antiqued with burnt umber.
2. Antiqued with alizarin red, burnt umber, and a little black for a softly shaded effect.

WHITE

1. Use raw umber and chrome green (easy on the green) to get a subtle charcoal shading with just a hint of green.
2. Two-thirds prussian blue, one-third ultramarine blue,

PLATE 51. This gilt decorator piece by the author has a fluted metal plate built into the topmost point of its center column to accommodate various types of bowels (see cover illustration), a fat candle, or fruit and flower arrangements. Here, a clear glass bowl is used with gaslight shades and long crystal prisms.

with a touch of black. If you like a blue and white look, this is for you. But do antique heavily in some places; in others, rub the mixture off, almost entirely exposing the white background.

3. White is lovely antiqued in gold (see "How to Antique with Gold," p. 159).

4. Or it can be antiqued in burnt umber.

OLIVE GREEN

Antique with burnt umber.

GOLD

To antique over gold (I use an enamel-base spray paint), *let it dry for a week*. Then add a coat of satin varnish *before* you antique with burnt umber—or the gold may turn dull and rub off.

YELLOW GREEN

1. Antique with viridian green, a little burnt umber, and a dash of black for an interesting monochromatic effect.

2. Antique with burnt umber for a muted chartreuse.

ULTRA TURQUOISE (BRIGHT)

1. Antique in burnt umber for dark green with a turquoise cast.

2. Antique in raw umber with a little black for a grayed turquoise.

PALE PINK

Pink looks muddy when antiqued in umber, but it is breathtaking done in alizarin red, with a little burnt umber and a dash of black. *Use a very pale pink for your background color.* Alizarin is so dominant that it may penetrate the pink paint slightly. To combat this, put a light coat of satin varnish over your pink background, and allow it to dry overnight before antiquing.

This way you can be assured of *pale pink highlights* in spots where all the antiquing mixture is wiped off, as well as *deeper pinks,* shading into *rich deep burgundy* where it is antiqued the heaviest.

The large lamp in Plate 52 was painted in dark and light tones of the same color—ultra turquoise (deep) at the base, merging gradually into Newport blue (light) about two-thirds of the way up. (Two brushes, one for the light and one for the dark paint, were used in blending.) The entire lamp was then antiqued in raw umber with a little black added.

Varnishing

After your antiquing has dried overnight, the final step is a coat of low-gloss varnish. (The duller it is, the better it will look.)

Do not shake the can, but stir gently to avoid bubbles. Set the can in warm water.

Lint is the thing most apt to ruin a good varnish job, so choose a time when the house is quiet and people are not moving about. Then, before you start, use the palm of your hand to rub over the article you're going to varnish, and blow on it to remove any trace of lint.

PLATE 52. Decorative pieces by the author. The oversized table leg lamp with a metal base is two shades of turquoise, antiqued in umber and black. The chartreuse potpourri jar, as well as the wall hanging which is brown and turquoise, and the walnut-finished lavabo have a touch of brass trim.

Flow on warm varnish with a light-bristled varnish brush, keeping an eye out for runs.

How to Antique with Gold

This is a very old and excellent method for antiquing with gold.* It is beautiful over white paint—gloss or semigloss. (This is one place a gloss paint works very well since it withstands rubbing better and will tone down anyway, after it is antiqued.)

You will need a small container of bronzing powder (light gold—or for copper tones, deep gold or brushed brass). Now mix equal parts of ordinary paste floor wax and satin varnish. Put two tablespoons of each in a shallow can. Set the can in a pan of hot water. When the wax melts, stir it into the varnish. (The mixture can be kept warm in the hot water or allowed to cool if it seems too fluid.)

Next, using a small cloth, dip it first in the wax-varnish mixture, then in the powdered gold, and rub it over the painted surface. In places the gold will partially wipe off, clinging here and there to give an antiqued look. If too much gold adheres, rub briskly with a clean cloth, or use a little paint thinner. At any stage in the operation, if you are not pleased with the results (up to the point where your antiquing is completely dry), it can be cleaned off, with thinner, and redone.

But once you've achieved the desired effect and allowed the wax mixture to dry completely, that's all there is to it—you need not even cover with varnish. It has been my experi-

* Do not use this formula on ornate or deeply carved designs. This particular process is better suited to plain pieces with smooth, rounded contours, giving them an effect of aged wood with a patina of gold.

ence that this type of antiquing is more permanent and less apt to darken later than some of the ready-mixed wax golds now on the market. A white lamp that I antiqued five years ago in this manner has retained its original golden look with no trace of tarnish and without any added protective coating.

Alternate Methods of Applying Gold

1. On ornate pieces or high-relief designs, spray-paint with gold; let dry for a week before varnishing. Allow varnish to dry overnight; then put a thin coat of white over it, and rub off on the high spots to leave a suggestion of gold showing through.

For a more mellow look, add a coat of varnish, let it dry overnight, and antique with burnt umber antiquing mixture, leaving umber only in deepest areas of design.

2. If you don't particularly want an antiqued effect, but more of a white and gold look, buy an inexpensive bottle of liquid gold (paint store, hobby shop, or variety store). Shake well, and use a small, very dry brush. (Remove most of the gold from your brush by drawing it once or twice across a piece of paper.) Then, gently but quickly, swish your brush over the high spots of the design. Restraint is the secret. Too much gold may bubble the paint underneath and, in any case, will detract from the total result.

If tole or decorative painting classes are available in your area, it might be worth your while to take a few lessons—if only for the antiquing. Each teacher offers distinctive touches and color techniques that might answer your problems as they arise and perhaps save you unnecessary effort.

One last word in regard to finishing your treasures: Don't become so intent on attaining perfection that the joy of *doing* escapes you. A case in point is the lamp in Plate 23, which I put together and painted some years back with a good deal more enthusiasm than skill. Using the proverbial hit-or-miss method and some brown paint (spatter-dashed on the lamp with a comb and an old brush), I achieved an effect of sorts, antiquing much of the basement and most of myself in the process. Oddly enough it all came under the heading of fun, because creating is its own reward.

II

Creative Ways to Use
Ordinary Things

WHENEVER a tour of your usual shops fails to turn up easily recognized treasure, a little imagination applied to everyday items may uncover a wealth of inexpensive material.

The potpourri jar in Plate 19 was made from the bottom section of an aluminum silex coffeepot. (In a moment, I'll tell you how to rejuvenate these, as well as what to use for lids.)

Two angel-food-cake pans in graduated sizes form the three-tiered compote in Plate 53 (left), while the fluted one on the right was once a pair of Jell-o molds. Incidentally, a pair of salt and pepper shakers were built into this one as part of its center column—one in the stem directly above the base, the other atop the lower pan. All the coffeepots, cake

PLATE 53. Finished in antique red, these double-tiered compotes made by the author are constructed from angel-food-cake pans and Jell-o molds.

pans, and Jell-o molds were found in the "as is" department, as were the thinly plated metal-alloy shakers.

With tops removed and holes drilled in the bottoms, salt and pepper shakers such as these, or even the plainer ones, make good building parts. Although I wouldn't recommend their use in a lamp, they are sturdy enough for this type of lightweight piece.

The clue to building with angel-food pans or Jell-o molds is the generous use of *rimmed* metal rings (either seating or check rings, since flat metal washers are inclined to slip out of place here). Don't forget that such rings can often be salvaged in the "as is," and they are necessary for this kind of building material in order to reduce the pans' center holes down to lamp rod size. By studying Figure 11, you can readily see why your finished pieces might be unstable without them.

To get back to our silex potpourri jars, the handles on the original coffeepots are nearly always attached by a metal band encircling the neck. To remove, clamp the handle in a vise, and work the coffeepot back and forth till the band snaps. (Sometimes, the handle can be removed by simply unscrewing two tiny locknuts.) This means there are no holes left to be covered, and the coffeepot, minus its handle, not only has a remarkably pleasing shape, but also makes a practical container for any number of things—my favorites being cologne-scented cotton or powdered sachet to lend elusive fragrance to a room.

As for the lids on the transformed jars (Figure 12), one consists of a single metal part added to a decorative piece of wood (Plate 8, Number 12). The other one (Figure 12b) was put together according to the basic method—a few parts strung on a rod. In each case the rod was a long threaded bolt, which happened to fit perfectly—in terms of threading—that

FIGURE 11. How parts were strung on the rod to assemble the cake pan and Jell-o mold compotes in Plate 53.

is, inside the lower end of the fancy knob, or finial. (Finials are threaded for various sized rods, from very small to floor lamp size.)

As the diagrams show, all three lids have lower extensions which fit down into the narrow necks to provide a neat closure. Notice that each lid is constructed from entirely different parts. This brings up a point. There must be liter-

FIGURE 12. a. Simple wooden lid for potpourri jar has lower extension to fit down inside jar. This lid was made from the piece of wood shown in Plate 8, Number 3. b. Method used in assembling lid for potpourri jar shown in Plate 19.

ally hundreds of ideas along this same line that could, conceivably, be worked out.

Right now might be the best time to mention a few tips on painting and antiquing these jars—they're so round that it's a little like trying to hold a ball and paint it, too. However, I've found the following method satisfactory: Place your left hand inside the coffeepot (if you are right-handed), and turning it upside down, paint the bottom and sides clear to the flat part of the rim where the lid will eventually rest.

In the second stage, the rim is painted down far enough inside the jar so that no line of demarcation is visible. Below that point I leave the coffeepot's aluminum finish, although it can be painted inside if you prefer.

The antiquing is done in one process to assure a unified result. Start the same way you did for painting, left hand inside, doing the bottom and sides to the rim. But since the center bottom of the potpourri jar will never be seen (unless it is picked up and examined), gently wipe off some of the antiquing mixture in a small central area there, not waiting for it to dry. Now, set the still-damp jar on a paper towel to finish applying the antiquing mixture on the flat part of the top rim and down inside the neck.

The paper towel serves to hasten your drying process so that by the time you are ready to rub off the excess antiquing elsewhere, the bottom area won't mar (provided you move it about on the towel as little as possible).

Another delightful bit of creativity is the colored glass window that I mentioned in Chapter 3 (Plate 54), the one a friend made for her apartment from bits and pieces of colored glass. As an adhesive she used ordinary household cement—the kind you can buy in almost any store.

Her very practical method of installing the finished window is one of its most ingenious aspects. We'll go into that, too, but first let's see how the window itself was put together.

In the entryway of her apartment is a tall, narrow window with small leaded panes, and its overall dimensions are sixteen by thirty-four inches. She had a piece of glass cut exactly to these measurements so that the finished window could be superimposed *over* the original glass, thus giving an illusion of being set in the window frame.

The next step was to work out, on a piece of paper cut the same size as the glass, a design of sorts—nothing too specific or formal, just the suggestion of a flower with stem and leaves— and this provided a pattern to follow in arranging colors.

She had for some time been saving glass, broken and otherwise—in all shades of green, blue, and turquoise, as well as red and amber—salvaging broken objects of colored glass, as

PLATE 54. Colored glass window created by Loraine Summers. It was constructed on a clear glass windowpane from bits of broken colored glass. Featured in the hallway of her apartment, the window is executed in shades of blue, green, and turquoise, with touches of warmer reds and yellows. The window's background color is a rich deep amber.

well as collecting bottles, plates, and bowls from secondhand stores. Before she started to work on the project, all the glass was carefully washed. After this it was put in paper bags (one color per bag) and placed on her cement-floored patio, where the bags were given a few whacks with a hammer until the glass was in fairly small pieces. Naturally, the result was a variety of shapes and sizes, including tiny bits and slivers that were later utilized to fill in open places in the design.

Each paper sackful of broken glass was segregated according to shade and color, then placed in small separate boxes alongside the pane of glass with its outlined paper design underneath. (For this project she set up two card tables.) The only other material used was household cement, six tubes for a window this size. After some preliminary experimenting, she applied glue generously to each piece of colored glass, but not all over, just to the high spots which would come in contact with the pane of glass. (Gloves and tweezers were discarded as being too much bother.)

Although this is a delightful project, it is also a very painstaking one and cannot be rushed. Don't plan on turning out a finished window in an afternoon—or in two. So set up your enterprise where it will be undisturbed and you can work whenever time allows. (My friend did hers in a spare bedroom.)

To assemble this kind of art window is like doing a jigsaw puzzle—you hunt and hunt for the right piece of glass to fill in each odd-shaped space. Incidentally, my friend's entire design was built up (including the background of amber glass) as she went along. For some, however, it might be easier to do the design first, filling in the background portions later.

When you've finished, even if you fill in remaining fissures or crevices with bits and splinters of colored glass, there are bound to be tiny lines of clear glass still showing through here and there. Surprisingly, these do not detract, but rather enhance the effect, serving to outline your design.

A window is set in place with its rough side (the side with the glass glued on it) facing inward toward the other window-pane, thus eliminating any dust-catching surfaces. To hold the glass there, a heavy-duty spring type of curtain rod is snapped into position against opposite sides of the window casing and snugged up close to the smooth side of your colored window —one at the top, another at the bottom.

One more thing: Specify *crystal* when you have your pane of glass cut. Even double-strength window glass might be a trifle light for supporting the additional weight. Better not attempt an overly large window either. Dimensions may vary somewhat, but this is approximately the area of glass that won't be unduly hard for you to handle.

There are many ways of using ordinary materials unconventionally, and following are a few suggestions:

Small sturdy steel springs—with a seating ring glued to one end—can become candleholders in the modern manner. (There is no reason you can't build pieces that are contemporary in style if your taste happens to lean that way or if you are planning a gift for a friend who likes modern décor. See Plate 7.)

The plaster statue which was converted to a candleholder (Plate 55) was an "as is" purchase. After a large chip on one side was mended, a wooden salad bowl was attached to its top. Then the entire piece was painted and antiqued.

Occasionally, there will be old machinery gears or wheels which are quite pretty. (See Plate 14, Number 5.) These can be scrubbed up and used as part of a lamp or candlestick.

The elaborate decorator piece in Plate 56 has a fluted

PLATE 55. Contemporary piece by Carol Simmons. A plaster statue found in a secondhand store has been converted into a candleholder. The statue is painted olive green, antiqued heavily in umber. The candle and fruit are in shades of yellow and coral.

PLATE 56. This gilt floor piece by the author measures almost five feet in height, is constructed of heterogeneous materials—all secondhand—including parts made of cast iron, pot metal, wood, and brass. A metal lid serves as the large candleholder.

cast-iron valve handle built into its elegant pedestal. And each of the six upright spindles on the compote candelabrum shown in Plate 38 includes a small machinery gear—I once found a whole box of them in the "as is."

Metal belts or chains may be used for added interest or decoration and are invaluable for covering imperfections— as in the lamp shown in Plate 23, the top part of which was originally a small bucket, and where its handle had been removed, the enamelware was chipped.

Small-nosed pliers were used to open links in a decorative metal belt and to reclose them around the neck of the bucket. Such a belt, if used in this manner, must fit snugly on whatever object it is to beautify. Here is how this is accomplished: Open a link, and remove approximately the length of chain or belt you will need. Reclose the link so that the belt encircles the object. Next, take the pliers, and going around your chain, squeeze the metal links together gently, tightening a link here, a link there, till all the slack is eliminated.

Lengths of brass chain from a bracelet ornament the potpourri jar in Plate 19. Buttons and metal jewelry, if applied with glue or epoxy, will provide excellent camouflage for holes. And brass paper fasteners can also be used anywhere that the prongs can be turned back on the underside without showing, for instance, on a base. Twist each prong slightly with small-nosed pliers until the head of the fastener is firmly in place. Add a spot of glue or epoxy to the prongs, and prop the base upside down until dry.

When you prefer to cover a hole without ornamentation so that the mended spot remains flush with the surface, products such as liquid solder, liquid aluminum, liquid steel, and so on will do an excellent job. (But don't rely on these for joining pieces of metal or parts.)

Let's assume you have a metal base with an unnecessary hole in it which is a little larger around than the head of a thumbtack. From the *underside* of the base, place a small patch of masking tape over the hole (sticky side showing through the hole). With the base right side up, squeeze liquid solder from the tube in a thin layer to overlay the masking tape and to fill in the hole topside. Prop the base at the proper angle so that the solder will be level and not run off. Let it dry thoroughly; then peel off the tape underneath, adding a bit more solder over your first application if the mend seems fragile.

Miraculous new products for all sorts of repair jobs continue to appear in the stores. For instance, in addition to epoxy glue, a variety of products are now being marketed—epoxy cement, steel, aluminum, and so on.

The marvelous thing about this group of epoxies is that you can repair castoffs that would otherwise be unusable. The jewel box in Plate 12, for example, not only was minus a hinge pin, but also had a wide crack up one side and a hole in a lower back corner. By filling in the crack with two applications of epoxy cement, allowing one to dry before the second was added, and then by sanding till smooth, this elegant little box was saved from the junk pile. When it was relined with pale blue silk and given a coat of white paint antiqued in gold, no one would know it had ever been mended. The pair of candlesticks in the same plate was assembled from a variety of small parts and then painted to match. A final fillip was added by choosing candles of a color to match the jewel box lining.

To reline one of these decorative boxes, first cut two narrow strips of thin cardboard, one as long as the inside circumference of the box and wide enough to fit under its lip or

How to Make Something from Nothing

rim. The other, very narrow indeed, goes on the inside rim of
the lid. With these, form oblong rings by gluing ends together
so that one fits nicely inside the box and one in the lid.
Should your jewel box still contain its original lining, remove
it carefully, and use it as a pattern.

Sometimes you can line these boxes without cardboard by
simply adding glue a little at a time, then poking the turned-
under edge of material up under the box's rim, using a
spoon handle or the blunt end of an orangewood stick. If you
prefer this method of lining, you'll find it easier to insert the
cotton after the silk has been partially glued into place.

Otherwise, place cotton inside the lid and in the box to
create a padded effect under the silk; then fit silk-covered
cardboard circlets into place, and glue just enough to hold.

For mending jobs in which you need to fill in a hole of
some depth, crumple bits of aluminum foil, pack it into the
hole, and then fill with epoxy cement.

To simplify any job of gluing or mending, one of the
handiest things you can buy is a flexible palette knife. I find
one indispensable when I blend my antiquing mixture and
when I mix or apply such things as epoxy, liquid solder, glue,
putty, or whatever. Be sure to clean the knife, though, the
minute you're through.

In order to disguise obvious construction details, fill in the
grooves on any exposed screwheads with epoxy cement or
liquid steel. The screws will then look more like pegs or
rivets and will contribute greatly to the handcrafted look,
particularly when they are antiqued.

Now, let's talk about brass. Suppose you are planning a
brass centerpiece and have accumulated all the necessary
parts. There is just one problem. The only base you have
that is the proper size or shape happens to be cast iron, instead

of brass. You can have it plated, and quite reasonably, too. The base of the compote in Plate 57 is cast iron, covered over with brass. Part of the base is rough, and part of it smooth, resulting in a combination of both dull and highly polished brass. This ties in perfectly with the crown-shaped compote bowl which also has a two-toned effect.

And while we're discussing the decorative qualities of brass, have you thought of inserting brass parts or pieces in painted objects? It is usually best to do the painted parts, as well as any antiquing, while your project is disassembled. Combine these later with the brass pieces which have previously been buffed or polished. The contemporary candelabrum in Plate 7 has a painted base and top, while the candle cups and midsection are brass. Of course, this same treatment can be used on pieces from any period.

The brass brackets from which light sockets dangled on old electrical fixtures (shown in the "before" picture in Plate 14 can be used as ornamental touches in various ways —for instance, on a table leg sconce (Frontispiece, Part III) or sometimes as an arm bracket.

If you don't intend painting a brass piece, yet it has deeply tarnished spots, commercial buffing is the only answer. (Look in the yellow pages under "Metal Polishing" or "Plating.") This also holds true for copper, which is even more subject to corrosion than brass.

However, you'll find some pieces of brass that are in moderately good condition underneath a coat of paint. Others, which haven't been painted over, may look shabby because of scratched lacquer that has yellowed or is sloughing off. On pieces such as these, you can do a fair job of restoring them at home.

First, strip off any lacquer or paint, using either sal soda or

PLATE 57. This brass compote made by the author is owned by Margaret Haydon. The compote bowl is part of an old commercial lighting fixture turned upside down. Ten such fixtures, minus their glass shades, were found at an electrical store's closeout sale. A smaller fixture of identical design is built into the decorator piece in Plate 56.

PLATE 58. Gaslight shades s⸢e⸣ on bases of polished brass b⸢y⸣ Loraine Summers. The bra⸢ss⸣ chain used as trim is fro⸢m⸣ junk jewelry.

lye. (See Chapter 10.) Do it quickly. Don't allow them to soak long, or they will become very dark and require buffing. Even so, when the pieces have been rinsed, tarnished areas will appear. If only surface-deep, these can be removed by rubbing over them with a cloth dipped in vinegar and salt (plenty of salt). It will cause the brass to turn slightly pink, but this will disappear with a little polishing.

Don't prolong the vinegar-salt treatment, and rinse quickly and thoroughly afterward with water. Then let it dry, and polish it with a good cream or paste brass polish. The paste kind which comes in a tube is excellent, and I buy it at a sporting goods store. (They use it to shine spinners.)

This done, you can have your brass lacquered or do it yourself. Metal lacquer for this is available in paint stores, though I bought mine at a plating shop. Use a light-colored, not too thick one. And always work in a well-ventilated room —the fumes may be irritating.

Metal lacquer is somewhat tricky to apply, since you must keep watching for runs, yet flow it on quickly and evenly with an absolute minimum of brushing over a second time. Have the brass slightly warm to begin with, and after the pieces are lacquered, set them in front of a warm oven. (They dry very rapidly.)

Brass parts can be lacquered either before they're assembled or after. I usually find it more efficient if they are done beforehand; especially if I plan to use them for building a rather large piece. Be sure to guard against scratches, however, particularly after it has been lacquered.

Brass varies in color, ranging from yellow tones to a coppery gold. This presents a problem if you're hunting for parts that will blend to appear as if they are one piece. Personally, I'd just as soon mix them a bit. Sometimes a slight variation in color can be quite interesting.

Glass furnishes a lovely complement to polished brass. And an endless array of combinations is possible. A few are shown in Plates 58, 35, and 34.

When you are having brass commercially buffed, and you want to avoid an overly shiny, dime store effect, ask to have it oxidized slightly. This makes any piece of brass look more like an antique, especially where there is an embossed design.

You can even do this yourself, before it's lacquered, by darkening just the deeper areas of a design with a tiny brush dipped in liver sulfate. (It has an unpleasant sulfurous odor, so I'd advise doing this out of doors or in the garage.)

By observing the few precautions mentioned here, you'll find brass a pleasant change of pace in your building. It will accent any décor and overcome the sameness of having all painted pieces.

I2

This May Be for You

CREATING treasures from the junk pile inevitably leads to an overabundance of decorator pieces, because there's always just *one more project that you want to try*. When my own hoard had become a problem, I knew I'd soon have to give up junking or clear some of it out. A friend whose enthusiasm for building had also exceeded her available space suggested that we combine our creations and sponsor an open house sale.

We chose a date three months away because that would give us time to complete projects already under way and a chance to use up some of the building material on hand. At that time, gaslight shades were very plentiful. And our specialty was a rather simple combination—a low base consisting of nothing more than a brass flange with a pretty, clear glass shade set on top and a metal part to hold the vigil cup inside the shade. (See Plate 58.)

For our open house, we assembled a few larger pieces as well—wall sconces, brass compotes with milk-glass bowls and vigil cups, and a few black iron hanging pieces. (One thing we learned from our sale—people's taste in decorative items varies considerably, so it's a wise idea to keep this in mind if you are building to sell.)

The genuine interest in our newfound handicraft was surprising, and when it came time to count up the proceeds, though our percentage of profit was modest, we had a little money to reinvest in more material and enough left over to buy some new accessories.

Since then, I've heard about a woman in Paris, who makes a living out of originating new ways to use old things. She travels all over France, buying old and secondhand objects, then hires craftsmen to rebuild or transform them. While an elaborate commercial project of this sort does not appeal to me, once a year, at Christmastime, I select a few of the pieces I've built that are decorated in a holiday mood, and a local antique store handles them for me. Their newspaper ads go something like this: "Featuring Ruth Egge's Christmas Accessories—made from old things." A similar arrangement might be possible with dealers in your community. It's worth thinking of, at any rate, and would provide a little extra for splurging on the family gift list.

To go back for a moment to an open house sale—it also works well on a once-a-year basis. Mrs. R. Simmons, a young homemaker with a husband and two children, likes this method because it gives her a chance to plan ahead and prepare for it.

Her father, who is retired and lives nearby, does the actual assembling of the pieces. But first, Mrs. Simmons designs them, deciding what parts go well together and in general how each will look when finished. And after her father has constructed them in his basement workshop, she takes over the painting and antiquing. The finished products are stored in her roomy attic until needed.

Some of her friends work on similar projects of their own, then pool their talents for the show. The day before the big event, they all pitch in to decorate the pieces with candles, fruit, flowers, pine, holly, and so on. The prices at the sale, however, are so reasonable that all items are priced without the accessories. This is understood ahead of time, and no one seems to mind. Two large clothes baskets are placed in a spare room, and all accessories are emptied into them. When a container is sold, making available some of the choicer accessories, another centerpiece may be whisked into the back room and redecorated by one of the participating hostesses.

The mechanics of such a sale are quite simple: A numbered master list is drawn up, including a description of each article, its price, and the seller's name. Pieces are then tagged, one by one, with a masking-tape tab on which are written the number, price, and initials of the seller. On the day of the sale a strip of quarter-inch plywood (about twelve inches wide and three feet long) is used as a check board. When each decorator piece is sold, its masking-tape tab is removed and stuck on the board. At the sale's conclusion these small adhesive tabs are taken from the board and placed in corresponding position on the list, eliminating any possible confusion.

Every year this show draws an amazing number of people, and sales are brisk. (As with most hobbies that prove fascinating, Mrs. Simmons tells me she invariably pours the pro-

ceeds from her sale back into more junk and accessories.)
Though you'd imagine that everyone attending would be inspired to hurry home and launch similar building projects,
many people prefer to buy these things already made. Hap-
pily for them, as well as for the do-it-yourselfers in this world,
there are those who find creative expression in baking a pie
or tailoring a suit or planting a garden.

For those who enjoy working with their hands, junking
can either be a profitable hobby for themselves or to further
fund-raising projects of church, school, and other organizations. The contribution of a lovely lamp or some particularly
dramatic decorator piece constructed from salvaged materials
is always welcome and usually adds substantially to the sale's
proceeds.

Age is no deterrent to proficiency in junking, and residents
of retirement communities throughout the country may find
it a stimulating way to supplement fixed pensions. Senior
craftsmen in many cities have even joined in cooperatively
operated shops. As a rule, these are sponsored by a nonprofit
organization, which takes the craft products on consignment
from the individual, then pays operating costs out of the
small commission charged. (The increasingly popular flea
markets are run along similar lines, except that individuals
or organizations set up their own display tables, paying a fee
for this privilege.)

To my mind, however, the real pleasure in this hobby lies
in discovering new ideas. That's why I haven't gone seriously
into the commercial side of junking. I leave this challenge
for those of you who are intrigued by its potential.

Incidentally, if selling doesn't appeal to you, have you ever
considered the possibilities in trading? The idea has been
suggested to me a number of times by people who favor this

method—trading either materials or services. With the latter, both parties stand to gain, since you are actually exchanging labor which is at a premium right now.

I have bartered my handiwork for marvelous attic junk, furniture, art supplies, and books, as well as some highly appreciated services—among them dressmaking, housecleaning, photography, and even yard work by a man who coveted a particular candlestick as a gift for his wife, then later decided he had to have some lamps, too.

Anyway, you can see why a hobby grows and expands—and why each individual finds in it something different and satisfying.

Part IV
LET YOURSELF GO

13

Accessories

Now for the frosting on the cake. Accessories. These are
extras—things to make and things to buy that will provide a final touch of inspiration no matter what your décor.

First, let's consider accessories that you might buy to set off
some recently finished decorator piece. It may be nothing
more than a candle in a lovely shade or a cluster of trans-
parent grapes. It might be a few flowers, a pretty glass bowl,
or even prisms—I have one friend who added long crystal
ones to her wooden candelabrum. (Plate 6.) To attach
them, she used six small screw-eyes (the kind used to fasten
wire to the back of a picture frame). Since these are threaded,
they can easily be screwed into the wood, and such tiny loops
show very little—even less after they've been painted along
with the candelabrum. The nice thing about this is that the

clear crystal prisms can be left off entirely for a change, or colored ones can be substituted on a special occasion.

Prisms, of course, are available in a sparkling array of shapes and colors. It's easy to imagine the many variations they suggest—especially when it comes to coordinating color schemes. For example, if green is the color you want to accent, use green prisms (with green vigil cups or candles). Or to pick up shades of lavender and purple, add amethyst ones.

Don't overlook the decorating magic in colored vigil candles. For a start, try a pink candle in an amethyst cup. It gives a deeper, prettier shade to the glass. Yellow candles in turquoise cups produce a greenish aqua color, blue candles in green cups a blue-green effect, and so on—all very striking.

In bright sunshine or candlelit rooms, glass is such a lovely reflector of light. So, do consider the use of glass bobeches, cup-shaped or flat ones with holes from which prisms are suspended (like those used on crystal chandeliers). There are all kinds of inexpensive ones, and often you'll find them on secondhand pinup lamps. It's surprising how effective these little glass bobeches can be, if they're used creatively. You can build them right into your pieces.

The key to building with glass is to use plenty of those metal rings with rolled edges (seating or check rings—again, flat metal washers won't do, since they are apt to chip the glass). For very fragile glass middles—or columns—a felt washer inside the seating ring is an advantage.

Take special care when adding glass parts to a metal base. For example, on the glass floor candlestick (Plate 59), where its cast-iron base comes into contact with the glass upper structure, a felt washer has been inserted to provide cushioning between the two.

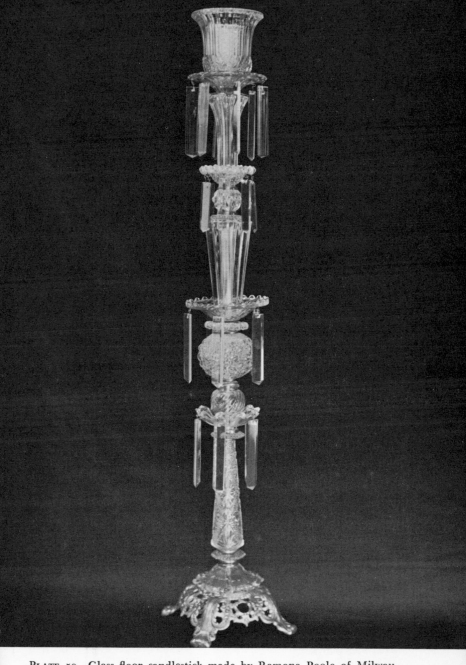

PLATE 59. Glass floor candlestick made by Ramona Poole of Milwaukie, Oregon. The crystal prisms were bought at an electrical store's closeout sale; the rest of the glass pieces were found on castoff pinup lights and table lamps acquired in junk shops or secondhand stores.

And now let me tell you about some of the glass pieces and the prisms that went into this lavish candlestick and where they were found. The owner of a local store specializing in hardware, electrical supplies, and lighting fixtures had sold the building and was in the process of liquidating his stock. (Such sales are often a junker's paradise, since most shops that specialize in light fixtures do their own assembly.)

Along with three of my treasure-hunting friends, I spent the better part of a delightful week, making trip after trip to the sale, poking into corners or exploring the loft. Purchases included material—whole cartons of unused light fixture pieces and building parts, as well as a lot of crystal prisms in varying lengths. These were considered the find of the day by one of my friends who is an ardent admirer of French Provincial décor, and it was she who built the elegant glass candlestick. A few of the middle parts for her candlestick were also acquired at the sale, but the glass bobeches—both the petal-shaped ones and those that are somewhat flatter—she discovered in junk and secondhand shops.

Now, about *metal* bobeches. For an example of how these can be incorporated into your construction, see Plate 60. Once in a while you'll run across a metal bobeche among light fixture parts, or you can buy them at lamp stores. Around their rims, at evenly spaced intervals, there are tiny holes just big enough for a prism pin.

In Plate 61 the prisms are suspended from a metal flower, and the holes are at the tips of the petals. Notice also, in this same picture, that the gilt candelabrum is shown with small bowls, whereas in Plate 62 fluted gaslight shades and a candle are used instead.

Instant transformation. That's what I like best about having a variety of accessories—with them, you can achieve a

PLATE 60. Lamp by the author is red glass in combination with polished brass. It was assembled from secondhand material with the exception of the prisms and the metal bobeche from which they are suspended. The tole-painted tray on the wall is the metal lid from a cardboard barrel.

PLATE 61. This gilt decorator piece by the author is designed to hold small bowls, vigil cups, gaslight shades, or candles (see Plate 62).

PLATE 62. Triple-arm gilt candelabrum by the author is constructed from a floor lamp top, a table lamp base, plus assorted wood and metal parts. Shown here in a Christmas mood with artificial holly swag and milk-glass shades, the candelabrum adapts well to different accessories (see Plate 61).

different, seasonable look for any time of the year. Christmas, for instance—who can resist the urge to decorate? Plate 63 shows a table leg sconce dramatized by fir boughs (sprayed white) and clusters of grapes. Plates 64 and 65 demonstrate two ways of decorating candelabra for the holidays. In Plate 65 artificial leaves, small cones, and acorns are combined with tiny turquoise and green tree balls, the kind you buy in bunches at the dime store already attached to pipe-cleaner stems. For this sort of operation, the essential element is cotton-covered wire (also from the dime store). Available in white or green, it ties almost as easily as a piece of string and comes wound on a spool approximately the size of a medium-size spool of sewing thread. Another indispensable aid for making arrangements is florist's clay (see Chapter 2).

In using artificial greenery or flowers, clip the stems short with wire cutters; then wire together the stem end of one piece concealed in the foliage of a second. Snip short-stemmed bits from still another piece, and wire them in to make the foliage more dense. This facilitates tying it to your candelabrum, creating the effect of a casually draped Christmas swag.

Green and turquoise vigil cups are used on alternate branches of the candelabrum shown to accent the arrangement. Incidentally, vigil cups are available in a variety of kinds, colors, and shapes. The gaslight shades in Plate 28 are only one example.

Although these shades are not as plentiful as they once were, you can still find them in antique shops and occasionally in secondhand stores. One of my favorite methods for utilizing such shades is on glass candlesticks. The idea did not originate with me. Perhaps you've seen antique shades combined with glass candlesticks in this fashion. Here, on the West

PLATE 63. Sconce by the author, gold Madonna by Ilene Egge. The table leg sconce (Plate 15) is decorated here with gold and chartreuse artificial grapes and fir boughs sprayed white. The glass candlestick and vigil cups are chartreuse.

PLATE 64. This twenty-five-inch tree candelabrum by the author has been decorated for a Thanksgiving table with artificial fruit in autumn colors.

PLATE 65. This tree candelabrum by the author is the same one shown in Plates 19 and 64. Here it is decorated in a holiday mood with tiny cones, acorns, tree balls, and an artificial bird. The colors are green, gold, and turquoise with touches of white.

Coast, they are sold as elegant antique decorator items called Candeliers.

Virginia Thompson, the woman who creates these lovely pieces, told me how one small idea led her to invent and patent an adapter. She had become interested in the old-fashioned gaslight shades which were too beautiful to discard, but which, because nobody knew what to do with them, gathered dust in attics and basements or waited unsold on antique store shelves.

Occasionally, at an antique show, a dealer would display a beautifully matched shade and candlestick, the shade perched precariously on top and the whole arrangement held together by Scotch tape or florist's clay. The effectiveness of these, despite the crudeness of the method, gave Miss Thompson the desire to find a way of combining these lovely misfits that would be both secure and artistic.

She designed an adapter and had a metal spinner make an experimental model. The next problem was to find a way of fastening it to a glass candlestick. She tried glue, cement and finally plastic—for a time it seemed this might be the solution. But an expert on plastics, whom she consulted, discouraged her. Returning to the premise that the fastener should not be too permanent a substance, she began again.

Suddenly, unexpectedly, she had it—paraffin! (The kind used to seal homemade jellies.) Poured warm into the candlestick and then allowed to harden, the wax was just temporary enough so that it could be removed, yet it held firm, adhered to the candlestick, as well as to the prongs at the base of the adapter, and it looked fine, too.

An interested friend persuaded Miss Thompson to get in touch with a patent attorney. Though it took almost three years to arrange an art patent, this proved to be good advice,

PLATE 66. Metal adapters are used here in combining a bowl and gas-light shade with glass candlesticks. The technique is described in Chapter 13. The candlestick and bowl at the left are turquoise; the adapter, satin-finshed brass. The lower part of the etched shade (*right*) is clear glass, while the top portion is blue-green. The shade is set on a green candlestick.

because dealers from up and down the coast, intrigued by the adapter's usefulness and not realizing it was patented, began to make reproductions at a great rate. Upon receiving notice from Miss Thompson's attorney, however, they stopped. And now, with almost a decade of time still remaining on the originial patent, the adapter is sold as an accessory in antique stores.

If Candeliers interest you, the simplest candlestick, clear or colored, short or tall, is a potential one (Plate 66). You may not have any gaslight shades among your material, but a small glass bowl—one with the right-sized base to fit into the adapter—can be used in place of a shade.

Wall hangings are another interesting accessory, and you can make them from no more than a few pieces of junk, plus your own creative ingenuity. Basically, the two wall hangings in Plates 20 and 33 are simply fabric with a casing sewn in the top and bottom and lamp rods inserted for weight and to maintain tautness in the material. The one with the picture is a printed linen towel (narrow black braid was glued on for accent). The second wall piece is a remnant of upholstery material with its vertical edges raveled as fringe. Ornamental links from a metal belt serve as hangers on both. Light fixture loops (the kind you can open with pliers) were screwed onto the tops of both decorative bottom sections. (See Figure 13.)

Small holes were clipped in the fabric casings and were then closed around the lamp rod.

The smaller of the two bottom ornaments—which fastened only at the center—has a brass design (from metal jewelry) superimposed to conceal the loop, and this is tacked to the fabric with a needle and thread.

For the towel picture wall hanging, several lengths of

Accessories

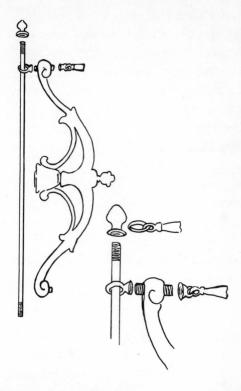

FIGURE 13. How the ornament is attached to the wall hanging in Plate 33. A rod is inserted at top and bottom of wall hanging.

small chain and metal tassels were added to the ornamental black pendant in order to give an illusion of greater width. These were used because, unlike the more delicate ornament on the other hanging, this heavier one appeared chopped off at the sides when attached to the wider picture towel. In Plate 3, Number 20, this same metal design is shown in its "before" state, and it would perhaps have looked better on a wall hanging of the same width, rather than on one so wide.

PLATE 67. Gaslight shade on a brass base by Loraine Summers. The small screen is finished in natural oak. It was designed by Carol Simmons and is made of carved wood from an old table. It forms an interesting background for an ever-changing combination of accessories.

PLATE 68. This planter lamp by the author is made from castoff brass pieces that have been stripped and polished. The lower portion of the base is natural wood.

(The extra center loop with metal bow was also put on as an afterthought to unify the design.)

Small paneled screens make an ideal backdrop for all sorts of arrangements. Plate 67 shows a four-panel screen made from the wide oak skirting around an old square dining table. (A carpenter cut and hinged the shaped panels.)

Shadow boxes, too, are a lovely way to display collections or floral whims. In Plate 40 you will see a shadow box that once housed a clock. When I found the case at a rummage sale, however, it not only was minus the clock, but also needed a new back and extensive regluing, as well as a few holes filled where metal fasteners had been removed. Transformed into a shadow box, this versatile piece is now one of my favorites.

The picture frame in the Frontispiece, Part IV, was once the front part of an old-fashioned cuckoo clock. On the back of the frame, at each side, are narrow grooved strips of wooden picture molding. These are fastened to the frame with glue and brads and notched, midway, to hold a wire standard (bent from No. 10 wire with a pair of pliers).

Incidentally, cuckoo clock faces are made in two sections, but it's a simple matter to join them together with glue and tiny brads.

Odd bits of metal, wood scraps, and unmatched glass shades or filigree gadgetry will inspire accessories as you experiment and build. Imagination is a personal thing—let yours work for you.

14

Lamps

WHEN you're creating a lamp, some of the most unlikely things can serve as construction material. The one in Plate 23 includes such unrelated items as an old stoneware crock, a floor lamp base, a small bucket with the wire handle removed, sections from a woman's linked metal belt, a Syrocowood ashtray (with a hole drilled in it), and a few other assorted parts.

It is quite possible that every lamp you build may be a combination of widely different substances, but painting and antiquing will make them all one. *Style, size* and *shape* are the important things to consider. So, before you set out to search for materials, take a trip through store lamp departments. Discover what type of lamp appeals to you—whether you are drawn to the quaint primitive style, the contemporary, French Provincial, or the Mediterranean. Find out if you like small lamps, massive spectacular ones, or a moderate in-between size. Do you prefer them plain and slightly rustic or extravagantly ornate?

If your choice is a big lamp, you naturally must gather some fairly good-size pieces. With that in mind, I selected a large base to begin the lamp in Plate 23. Casting about for a substantial piece to add next, I chose the crock because it had a hole in the bottom—not a neat round hole, but one that was rather jagged. Nevertheless, this made it possible to insert a lamp rod, and since the hole was concealed from view after being set onto the base, it really didn't matter.

If you want to build this sort of thing into a lamp, and there is no hole, you can have one drilled. (Otherwise, look for an old lamp part similar to the one in Plate 3, Number 16, or the one in Plate 8, Number 13.)

Incidentally, discarded table lamps can sometimes furnish you with a good beginning for a bigger lamp, especially if they're inclined to be rather large and bulky. All you need to do is get a longer rod, then add more parts on top of the original lamp. If the lamp is to be very tall, you may want to enlarge the base. Perhaps use the one that is already on the lamp, with another of greater dimension beneath.

You'll find a good many of these lamps will be plaster of paris, painted over. But they are adaptable. Surprisingly, many new ones in the stores today are also plaster of paris artfully camouflaged to look like wood or metal.

Sometimes a lamp constructed from this material will have the lamp rod imbedded in it so that only a short bit of rod extends above the lamp itself. You can add a threaded coupling, then another length of lamp rod in order to go on up and make a taller lamp.

Practically the only sort of part that isn't usable in building a lamp is one that's too thin or too fragile. (You must be able to turn the nut at the base end of your lamp till it is reasonably tight, so that all the parts will fit snugly one against another.) By fragile, I simply mean a piece made from something like thin brass or pot metal, which is so flimsy it will collapse at the slightest pressure. Most glass is durable enough, if rings are inserted between each piece. This brings up another point: Any *candlestick* you build that has a hollow rod through the middle (to contain the cord) can easily be turned into a lamp—for example, the glass candlestick in Plate 59, described in Chapter 13.

But let's suppose you've decided to build a lamp. Select a length of rod in accordance with the height of the lamp you intend to construct, and build nearly to its top, leaving the last half inch exposed—you should have room to add a harp and a light socket. (First the harp goes on the rod, then the socket.) See Figure 14a.

If you are inexperienced at lamp building, here is an alternative and perhaps easier way to assure having the proper amount of rod left over for wiring purposes: Build your lamp complete. Adjust all the pieces so they are straight; then add a nut, and tighten. Leave *an inch or more* of rod exposed at the top *after the nut has been tightened* and your lamp is sturdily secure. (One advantage of this method is that the main body of the lamp is steady, and the pieces won't shift out of line while you're working.)

Now return to your building material for a small part or parts—wood, metal or anything else that will fit over the rod and at least partially conceal the nut, but leave enough threaded rod exposed (half an inch or less) to accommodate a harp and a light socket.

You can buy the kind of light socket that works with a three-way bulb. Or if you want to make use of the sockets you have, there will surely be some ordinary ones in your secondhand material. One with a switch, instead of a chain, may be more satisfactory.

Open the socket. To do this, press on the casing near the lower portion, or cap, where it says "press." At the same time, flick off the cap with the blunt side of your screwdriver.

Slip a harp onto the rod. (Don't use too small a one.) Then screw the cap of the lamp socket on top to hold it in place, and the lamp is ready to wire.

This is really the best time to paint and antique your lamp, while there is no wire to get in the way. Besides, the harp can serve as a handle, enabling you to lift or move the lamp about while you do the antiquing. But whether you paint it now or after the lamp is finished, let's assume you are ready to proceed with the wiring.

Lamp cord is available by the foot. (When buying electrical supplies, check to see that they are marked with the Underwriter's Seal of Approval.) You will need a pair of kitchen shears or wire cutters, some small-nosed pliers, and a paring knife or a jackknife. Decide how long you want your lamp cord to be; then allow, in addition to this, a piece as long as the height of your lamp. It's much easier to cut off a little extra before attaching the wall plug than it is to add additional cord if you make it too short.

Thread the wire through the center of your lamp. The cord consists of two covered wires, each one made up of many fine copper strands. Divide the two main wires down the middle for about three inches. Scrape off the outer covering with your knife. Taking care not to cut through the copper

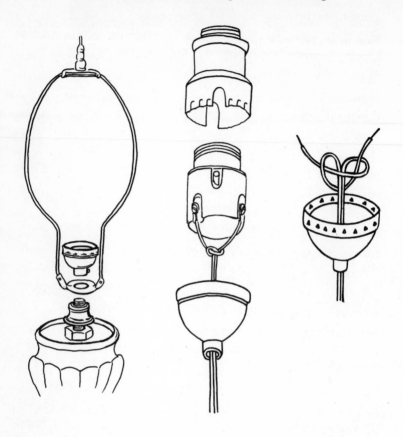

FIGURE 14. a. Add parts to top of lamp in this order. Thread lamp cord through lamp from underside of base. b and c. Strip ends of wire (see text). Tie knot in wire, and wrap ends around terminal screws as shown in c. Adjust cord from bottom of lamp (to take up any slack). Replace mechanism and casing in light socket cap.

strands, strip about an inch on both wires. Twist the copper strands together securely into two pieces.

Next, following the diagram in Figure 14c, tie an underwriter's knot (if you want to be exact), or any other sort of knot will do. Loosen the terminal screws (Figure 14b), and wind the wire closely around the screw shanks, clockwise. You may need to snip the wire shorter to make it fit well, but make certain that all copper strands are twisted tight again before proceeding. When the wire is firmly in position around the screws, tighten screws. Set both socket and casing down into the cap again, adjusting cord from the bottom of your lamp (to take up any slack).

Now for the wall plug: String the cord through the wall plug. Split the cord, and strip and prepare the wires just as you did before. Tie a knot, looping it around the prongs. Twist the wire around the terminal screws, and tighten the screws. Replace the cardboard prong cover over the wiring, and your lamp is finished, ready for use.

Space does not permit going into all the various steps involved in wiring multiswitch lamps. But you can build as intricate a lamp as you like—with small candlelights or special base lighting—so long as you remember to use hollow arms or provide somewhere for the cord to go.

If you prefer an ultrasimple method of wiring, you can buy do-it-yourself electrical supplies with clamp-on plugs and the like. There are even gadgets that can be fastened to the top of a lamp, eliminating the need to string wire through the lamp itself. These are called wired lamp adapters, but I favor wiring mine the conventional way.

The planter lamp in Plate 68 is all brass except for a wooden base. Note the fancy holder that covers the light socket. This finishing touch can be added to any lamp you build. (Holders come in various styles and are called chimney holders.) A socket fits down inside the holder, which has a hole on one side for the light switch. Unscrew the switch knob, and replace it after the socket is in place. Again, the harp goes on the rod first, then the holder, and finally, the socket.

Artificial greenery works out more successfully for planter lamps. If live plants are used, the soil will corrode the brass and ruin its appearance. It is equally damaging to a painted lamp with the planter feature.

Much more elegant in style is the lamp shown in Plate 60. Made of glass, deep red in color, combined with polished brass, this lamp is especially effective displayed in a window where there is plenty of light.

The ruby-colored glass came from several sources. The largest piece was once a vase. (A craftsman drilled a center hole in it for me.) All the rest of the glass pieces were collected from junk shop lamps of various shapes and kinds. They weren't acquired in a week or in a month, but eventually I found enough to build a lamp. The brass was also scavenged from discards, but the pieces were sufficiently usable to warrant having them buffed and polished. The prisms and the brass-plated bobeche from which they are suspended were the only parts that were not secondhand. These I bought in a lamp shop.

The main section of another lamp (Plate 52) is a wooden column that appeared to have belonged on a small pedestal table. When I found it in a junkyard, there was an awkward base attached. Removal of this disclosed a bolt set into the wood at the lower end. It was threaded and protruded from the post approximately four or five inches—made to order, I thought, for a candlestick.

To improve its shape, however, I sawed off a knobby section at the top and was surprised to find it hollow in the center. That's why it became a lamp, instead of a candlestick. After the bolt was unscrewed from the bottom end, there remained less than two inches of solid wood to be drilled. Beyond that a lamp rod would go all the way through.

As an indication of this lamp's size, observe the composite base. It consists of *two* floor lamp bases. Also, at the top of the lamp is still another base, a small ornate one from a table lamp, used upside down.

In regard to lamp parts, the upper section of a silex coffeepot is an adequate size to make a fine middle section for a large lamp, and luckily, there's already a hole through it. To adapt one of these, search through your material for a piece or part the right size to cover the top opening. (Lightweight metal lids with a center hole drilled in them will often work.) Then set the lower extension of the silex down into some other part that is large enough to conceal it. Used in this manner, the nicely rounded contours will give every appearance of having been specifically designed as a part of your lamp.

Do you begin to see why lamp building is such fun and why it is certain to start you thinking creatively?

15

Decorator Pieces

I T's only fair to warn you—if it isn't already too late—that once your ideas start to proliferate, it won't be long before you've come up with a design so impressive it inspires you to try one even more dramatic the next time. This in turn triggers another creative brainstorm that starts—well, I guess by now it probably is too late.

So let yourself go and come up with a real conversation piece—one that will be just right in that special corner by your own or perhaps a friend's front door. It does spur you on to finish a project if you have a particular place in mind for it. One such place once set my imagination to work and resulted in a truly extravagant creation.

A friend of mine lives at the top of a hill. The living area of her contemporary house is almost entirely open—one room flows into another—and high beamed ceilings soar outward beyond a window wall to form a roof for the deck beyond. Since the two of us have been on many a treasure hunt together, I knew just the sort of thing she had in mind when she remarked one day, "I'd love to build a really eye-catching piece to hold flowers and plants, either on the deck or out in the garden."

We were busily reconnoitering a secondhand store when she mentioned it, so the idea took hold at once—especially after I'd pounced on a large, but decrepit-looking, parrot cage which we decided might be the very thing to launch her Operation Spectacular.

Our other buys that day included an average-size birdcage with a better than average shape—Figure 15 shows the cage, as well as our second purchase, a stout wire plunger for washing clothes. Ordinarily this plunger wouldn't have rated a second glance, but sometimes one part will suggest another. And here was a piece that looked as if it might go well with our two cages, even though neither of us had the least notion *where* or *how*.

The small birdcage was in fine condition, but the pan at the bottom of the other was missing; this could have presented a problem. That could be solved later—the most obvious and immediate step was to give the parrot cage a thorough scrubbing in the laundry tray. Then, after a few of its "ribs" had been straightened with pliers, a spray coat of base paint was applied.

Next, we hung it from a basement rafter and began the trial-and-error process of designing. The smaller cage wasn't large enough to be effective without adding parts. But when the cages were put directly against each other, too great a con-

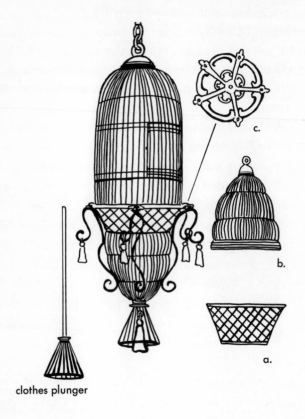

clothes plunger

FIGURE 15. Parts used in building the decorator piece in Plate 69.

trast in size was apparent, as well as a noticeable difference in the thickness of the wire.

Having already tried most of our likely parts without success, I dug through my reject box for alternate possibilities and found the latticed metal section shown in Figure 15a. This was once part of an old ceiling fixture, but it had been under my workbench for so long I can't recall now what it originally looked like. (I do remember that it was decorated with a lot of little metal flowers and leaves which I used in building the wall sconce described later in this chapter. See Plate 15.)

It was also my good luck to find the fancy star-shaped part shown in Figure 15c. Being lightweight pot metal, this was flat enough to serve as a bottom for the parrot cage. Then, too, it would make a place to set plants or flowers since the large cage had a fairly good-size door that opened.

Apparently, the only logical way to fasten this five-pronged piece underneath the big cage (without running a rod completely through the cage's middle) was to *wire* it into place. So we used small *flexible* wire from the dime store, twisted with the pliers until tight. And while we were at it, the latticed section was wired to the five-pointed piece.

At the time this seemed rather a makeshift method to me, but I've since concluded that it's very practical for any birdcage creation, because the wire blends into the background and is virtually invisible. After the finished piece has been spray-painted, it doesn't show at all.

Note, however, that there is a second way to construct birdcage spectaculars. Just drill a hole in the cagetop (or enlarge the one that's already there). Then use the lamp rod method. For example, you can build a floor-standing creation of similar design; but in this case, a rod extends from the topmost point of the cage all the way down and right through the center hole in the base. The rod, of course, is what holds the whole construction together.

As a matter of fact, this procedure was used on the *bottom section* of my friend's hanging piece, which consisted of the smaller cage turned upside down. We resorted to a lamp rod and strung various middles on it, not because we had to fasten it together, but because this type of construction seemed to improve our design. (The cage pan was eliminated and instead we set a metal plate—with a hole in the center—down into the cage.)

The rod was extended through the center of the smaller cage and finished off underneath the cage with our strange, but practical, buy from the secondhand store. Remember that old-fashioned clothes plunger? Well, the wire plunger had a small hole where the handle had been removed, so instead of making it bigger, we chose a threaded rod that was correspondingly small in diameter. A loop with threads inside was screwed on the rod at the lower end, but the metal tassel wasn't added until later.

By the time the bottom section had been wired to the lattice part, our design was beginning to take shape. It was then that we came up with the idea of the big tassel at the bottom, and the way it showed through the flared lines of the open wire plunger was pure inspiration.

Incidentally, these brass tassels—which are found in various sizes on many of the older fixtures—can be collected over a period of time and saved to use on just the right piece when it comes along. The five smaller tassels were attached with loops from a metal belt.

A hanging wrought-iron light fixture provided us with the five curlicued metal arms (used upside down). These were fastened by being wired (through small holes in the wrought iron) to the five points of the star-shaped part, which had been added earlier as a bottom for our large cage. Then, taking advantage of a second set of holes lower down in the wrought-iron arms, we wired them again. Only here, we added a tiny metal flower at each point of contact.

The long chain used to hang this decorator piece was found

in the "as is" section of the Goodwill. (The same result may be achieved by piecing together short lengths of chain from old light fixtures.) To attach our lengthy chain, we pried open one of the links (it's easier to do this in a vise), then pounded it shut around the loop at the top of the parrot cage.

And it was done.

Between us, we carried the rather weighty result (Plate 69) of our combined efforts outside, hung it from a tree, and sprayed it chalk white.

What a difference that paint made—the motley collection of parts blended as one into a summertime accent piece. A bit on the frivolous side? Perhaps. But it was built to be taken down in the fall—and destined to have a new coat of paint and fresh flowers as a lighthearted touch for spring.

I'm not sure the same gimmicks will work for everyone, but for me, at least, *time* can also be an incentive. Suppose you suddenly decide the centerpiece you've been building for the dining room table simply must be finished by a week from this Thursday because that's the day the bridge club meets at your house. With a deadline, it's amazing how much more keenly one's hands and brain will operate. It was this thought of a definite time limit that catalyzed me into building the big floor piece in Plate 56.

Christmas was almost here, and I was caught up in the hurry-scurry of holiday preparations. Relatives from out of town were expected momentarily, and there were a million things yet to do. Still, every time I passed my workshop on the way to the laundry room, I'd stop and try a few parts together, first one way, then another, in an effort to pin down my fleeting ideas. Time for it or not, the thought persisted. *It would be such fun to whip up something extra tall and really Christmasy to stand in that alcove by the fireplace.*

PLATE 69. Chalk white decorator piece made by Margaret Haydon. Built entirely from secondhand store bargains, this summertime piece is decorated here for a silver anniversary garden party. Fresh flowers are used in shades of pink, accented by white baby's breath and silvered ferns.

I chose a good-size base and a heavier, longer floor lamp rod. (The size factor seemed so important to me that after I'd built to the top of this one, I added a coupling and another section of rod to make it even taller.) Actually, assembling this piece was like building a combination candlestick, compote, and candelabrum all in one, but on a grand scale.

I sprayed my finished piece gold but decided the antiquing would have to wait until after Christmas. There just wasn't time for it.

The real fun with this let-yourself-go type of project comes when it's time to choose the accessories—things that will set it off to advantage, such as artificial fruit, flowers, greenery, or perhaps what I used in mine, poinsettias and fat red candles. After the holidays, I exchanged the red accessories for feathery green artificial ferns and turquoise candles to pick up the colors in my living room.

The same large-scale approach can be adapted to a less elaborate piece—more on the Early American order—and constructed by a method similar to that used on the wooden compote in Plate 38.

You will need two or more table legs, a base (probably from a floor lamp since the finished piece will be quite tall), and a large wooden salad bowl (for the compote part), plus a smaller one for the top. The steps used for putting it together (doweling and glue) are the same as that described in the chapters on wood.

The decorative wall sconce in Plate 15 wasn't built for a special occasion, nor was it assembled with any particular place in mind. My motivation was one of those lovely half table legs that a cabinetmaker had once cut for me. Remember—I told you about them back in Chapter 5. There is a hidden bonus in trying to find ways to use up such parts, because this is how new ideas are born.

To return to the sconce, however—it was assembled in the same general way as the one in Plate 36. But as you can see, there are features which make it more striking, such as the decorative candle cups and added wrought iron, also the lavish use of metal flowers and leaves. The old light fixture which had been fastened to the parrot cage was originally covered with them, and although you won't find fixtures like this every day, the flowers and leaves from old metal jewelry will look much the same after painting.

You can add as many arms as the piece will hold and substitute any kind of candle cup *so long as you're careful to stagger them, so they aren't directly in line with one another.* In that case, the candle's flame would be apt to scorch the candleholder above.

Here, by the way, is how I made a wall decoration before I ever thought of a table leg sconce. This one was haphazardly put together, but highly effective for Christmastime glamor. It was perhaps the forerunner of my later sconces. I made it by fastening a variety of arms from old light fixtures—seven in all—to a two-by-four about three feet long. These were crudely attached with screws, metal straps, nails—anything that would hold. But it didn't matter, because I wove fir boughs in and around the arms to cover the two-by-four completely, then sprayed the entire thing, fir boughs and all, a flat snowy white.

The candle cups were small—just the right size to hold tall dripless candles, instead of vigil cups—and the effect, when they were lighted, was breathtaking.

I used the decoration only at Christmas, with fresh fir boughs each year; then, after a time, I took it apart and rebuilt it into a permanent wall piece with a table leg back. That's a point to keep in mind, too. Change! Anything you make can be different. Somehow. Sometime.

The crystal and gilt creation with glass shades and prisms shown in Plate 51 is marvelous for decorating a buffet table. In fact, that's what inspired me in the first place. I'd been delegated to decorate a table for a local money-raising event, and of course, the challenge proved irresistible. This was truly a delightful piece to build because it turned out to be so astonishingly elegant. Yet it was put together the same way you would assemble a candlestick. Then the arms, taken from an old hanging fixture, were added as one complete unit (just like the ones that were built into the compote candelabrum in Plate 43). The candle cups on each of the five graceful arms were made to hold candles, small glass bowls, any kind of vigil cup, or gaslight shades. Do you recall how shades were adapted to wall sconces (in Chapter 8)? The same principles apply here.

The number and variety of decorator pieces that can be created are limited only by your imagination. So all those dilapidated and outdated pieces gathering dust in your attic really *are* too good to throw away. As La Fontaine said long ago, "A sensible person finds nothing useless."

Index

Numbers in italics refer to pages on which plates or figures appear.

Index